Transparent Leadership

Establishing a culture of trust in organizations and strengthening the middle line are both critical for implementing innovation, especially during major disruptions. Work units and teams operate in environments that are largely influenced by broader organizational and institutional goals where middle managers are most needed for guiding and directing the staff to carry out change.

Recently, however, the value of middle managers has come under attack. Despite their valuable contributions that often have gone unnoticed by senior executives, middle managers have regularly been viewed as non-value-added practitioners who consume resources but do not add value to products or services. Further, as technology advances and social media allow executives to interact more directly with stakeholders, it also removes middle management from the communication loops or the decision-making process.

Conscious about the potential of being eliminated, demoted, or bypassed, some middle managers attempt to "prove their premium" by working excessively hard, thus becoming hyper-effective, working longer hours with a desire to perform their roles better. Surprisingly, however, executives who react harshly to these attitudes and behaviors also typecast middle managers as being unmotivated and needed to be further bypassed or often incentivized monetarily to accomplish important tasks. Neglecting middle managers' strengths or focusing on negative attributes and weaknesses creates conditions of failure harmful to employees and organizations.

Transparent Leadership: Bridging the Trust Gap Between Senior Executives and Middle Managers focuses on trustworthy relationships between senior executives and middle managers. A proven framework of trustworthy leadership is presented as a practical guide for leaders and professionals wishing to gain skills for building and maintaining trust in the workplace. It provides practical strategies and assessment tools for bridging the trust gap between executives and middle managers.

Innovative Leadership Series

AI is rapidly transforming business strategies and leadership practices. Innovative leaders thrive by fostering continuous learning, collaboration, and empowerment, leveraging new technologies for organizational success. In high-stakes moments, clutch leaders make decisive, bold moves, and then promote shared ownership and co-creation to sustain engagement. Innovative Leadership emphasizes adaptability, purposeful innovation, and balancing stress with intuition and character. It combines expertise, empathy, and the "Why" with practical "Know-How" to promote growth. This three-book series equips strategists, executives, and managers with diagnostic tools to enhance self-awareness, leverage strengths, and achieve win-win outcomes amid disruption.

Books in the series:

Brilliant Leadership: Unlocking the Power of Innovation-Communication
Edited by Alan T. Belasen and Nicole Pfefferman

Forthcoming books in the series:

Clutch Leadership: Harnessing the Qualities of a Gamechanger
Edited by Alan T. Belasen and Barry Eisenberg

Transparent Leadership: Bridging the Trust Gap Between Senior Executives and Middle Managers
Alan T. Belasen and Ariel R. Belasen

Transparent Leadership

Bridging the Trust Gap Between Senior Executives and Middle Managers

Alan T. Belasen, PhD
and Ariel R. Belasen, PhD

Routledge
Taylor & Francis Group
A PRODUCTIVITY PRESS BOOK

Designed cover image: Shutterstock

First published 2026
by Routledge
605 Third Avenue, New York, NY 10158

and by Routledge
4 Park Square, Milton Park, Abingdon, Oxon, OX14 4RN

Routledge is an imprint of the Taylor & Francis Group, an informa business

Library of Congress Cataloging-in-Publication Data
Names: Belasen, Alan T., 1951- author | Belasen, Ariel R. author
Title: Transparent leadership: bridging the trust gap between senior executives and middle managers/Alan T. Belasen PhD and Ariel R. Belasen PhD.
Description: New York, NY: Routledge, 2026.
| Includes bibliographical references and index. | Identifiers: LCCN 2025040181 |
ISBN 9781041000679 hardback | ISBN 9781041000655 paperback |
ISBN 9781003608028 ebook
Subjects: LCSH: Middle managers | Industrial management |
Leadership Classification: LCC HD38.24.B45 2026
LC record available at https://lccn.loc.gov/2025040181

ISBN: 9781041000679 (hbk)
ISBN: 9781041000655 (pbk)
ISBN: 9781003608028 (ebk)

DOI: 10.4324/9781003608028

Typeset in Garamond
by Deanta Global Publishing Services, Chennai, India

Dedication

It is commonly thought that middle children tend to be more independent and self-reliant; they think outside the box, are more empathetic, and tend to feel less peer pressure due to a strong sense of self. Anat, my middle child, manifests these characteristics and more. She is a brilliant scientist who has recently completed two prestigious postdoctoral fellowships at Cornell University *and* UT Austin, respectively.

Anat completed her PhD in Ecology and Evolutionary Biology at the University of Michigan in 2019, focusing on the impacts of habitat fragmentation on amphibian health in the Brazilian Atlantic Forest biodiversity hotspot. She is now a Research Associate at UT Austin and maintains a research affiliation with the Smithsonian Center for Conservation Genomics.

Her accomplishments in STEM research, social justice, sustainability, and engagement with local communities in North and South America are exemplary. In 2005, when she was selected as the keynote speaker for her high school graduation, I suggested that she talk about the power of thinking outside the box. I still remember her response – "if everyone thinks outside the box, everyone is in the box," highlighting the paradox of convergent thinking, which limits creativity and exploration, negating the value and contribution of divergent thinking.

Divergent thinking is crucial for middle managers who navigate the complexity of disruptive innovation. It creates a sense of empowerment to explore unconventional approaches or identify new opportunities. It fosters a learning mindset for identifying innovative solutions and breakthrough possibilities that benefit organizations and communities and improve the quality of life.

From my middle child to the middle managers – Anat's high commitment to global change, wildlife disease prevention, biodiversity preservation, and social justice go beyond its intrinsic value. It significantly benefits humanity and the environment.

I dedicate this book to Dr. Anat M. Belasen.

Alan T. Belasen

Contents

About the Authors

Alan T. Belasen, PhD, is a professor, author, and leadership development consultant known for his work in corporate communication, healthcare leadership, and business education. A professor of management and corporate communication at SUNY Empire State University, Dr. Belasen has been instrumental in developing and leading several graduate-level business programs, including MBAs in management, global leadership, and healthcare leadership.

Beyond his academic work, Dr. Alan Belasen has extensive experience as a leadership development coach, trainer, and consultant. His consulting work has involved a diverse range of organizations, including private enterprises, nonprofits, and government agencies. His contributions to business education were recognized by the International Accreditation Council for Business Education's John L. Green Award in 2017.

Through his roles as an educator and consultant, Belasen has profoundly influenced aspiring and current leaders. His books, articles, and training programs have equipped managers with tools and strategies to navigate complex organizational dynamics, improve communication, and adapt to disruptive environments.

In addition to *Transparent Leadership* (2026), Belasen's other books include *Clutch Leadership* (2025); *Brilliant Leadership* (2024); *Transforming Leadership, Improving Patient*

Experience (2024); *Resilience in Healthcare Leadership* (2022); *Dyad Leadership and Clinical Integration* (2019); *Women in Management* (2017); *Confronting Corruption in Business*(2016); *Mastering Leadership in Healthcare* (2015); *Women in Corporate America* (2012); *The Theory and Practice of Corporate Communication* (2008); and, *Leading the Learning Organization* (2000).

Ariel R. Belasen, PhD, is a professor of economics recognized for his expertise in health policy, labor economics, econometrics, and applied microeconomics. He is respected as an innovative educator, researcher, and mentor who bridges academic excellence, applied policy, and student success. His career reflects a dedication to advancing knowledge at the intersection of economics, health policy, and social well-being, along with a deep commitment to preparing the next generation of global leaders.

He currently serves as the chair of Economics and Finance at Southern Illinois University Edwardsville. Additionally, Dr. Ariel Belasen serves as the Coordinator for Undergraduate Research and Creative Activities for the university, shaping the academic trajectories of countless students across all fields.

A passionate advocate for global learning, Dr. Belasen incorporates travel and real-world experiences into his teaching and research, drawing on his international background and love for cultural exchange. He has taught health economics and policy, managerial economics, and quantitative analysis for the MBA program as well as a variety of undergraduate business courses including courses in globalization and economic consulting.

As a researcher, Dr. Belasen has contributed or co-authored more than two dozen publications, including landmark studies on corruption, labor market shocks, health economics, and macroeconomic policy. Beyond academia, he worked as a

Research Analyst for the CMS Innovation Center at the Centers for Medicare & Medicaid Services, supporting policy research at a national level. His career also includes consulting engagements and quantitative research projects in public and private sectors.

Acknowledgments

I extend my profound gratitude to my wife, Lila, whose support has been indispensable throughout the time spent on this book. I would also like to thank my daughters Adina and Amira who motivate my daily productivity.

I offer further appreciation to my colleagues at Southern Illinois University Edwardsville, whose insights have been pivotal in shaping my understanding of how individuals and organizations face challenges.

Finally, and most importantly, thank you to my father, Dr. Alan T. Belasen. Your confidence in both me and this endeavor continues to serve as a persistent source of motivation and inspiration.

Ariel R. Belasen

This book benefited from the advice and insights of many colleagues from numerous networks and conferences including the Management Education and Development, Gender and Diversity in Organizations, and Healthcare Management Divisions of the Academy of Management. The anonymous reviewers of many journals helped extend my understanding of the complex interplay of leadership, influence, and accountability, with middle managers serving as a crucial link between the strategic vision of senior executives and the operational realities at the floor level. These include reviewers from *Gender in Management – An International Journal; Journal of Healthcare Management; International Journal for Quality in Health Care; International Journal of Strategic Communication; Journal of Health Organization and Management;* and the *Journal of Management Development.*

Special thanks go to my research partner and coauthor of this book, Dr. Ariel Belasen, Department of Economics and Finance, Southern Illinois University Edwardsville, whose collaboration with me on multiple research projects and journal articles spanning the value of middle management, executive performance, and leadership pipeline development have sparked important insights into the qualities of *Transparent Leadership* that are now infused throughout the book.

I am indebted to the coauthors of my previous books – Dr. Nicole Pfeffermann (*Brilliant Leadership*) and Dr. Barry Eisenberg (*Clutch Leadership*) – whose invaluable ideas and thought-provoking questions inspired me to think deeply about the complexity of disruptive leadership and disruptive innovation and significantly influenced the current book's development and final form.

I extend my heartfelt thanks to Dr. Lisa Vollendorf, President, Empire State University, and Dr. Rai Kathuria, Provost, for granting me the Sabbatical leave and the opportunity to extend my research on this book in support of my continuing growth. I am grateful to my colleagues at Empire's Business, Management, and Leadership program for the years of working together and sharing insightful ideas, many of which are explored in the book.

Many thanks to Kristine Mednansky, Acquisitions Editor, Taylor & Francis Group, who believed in the importance and relevance of this book project and was instrumental in moving this book project through the various production phases.

Many thanks to my wife Susan who supported the idea of collaborating with Ari to coauthor this book as the culmination of our many years of collaborative research and development. My other A's have always been supportive in ideas and inspiration – Amy, an accomplished author, founder of ABD Creative, Podcast host, digital marketing expert, and a successful travel blogger; Anat, PhD, Ecology & Evolutionary Biology, NSF Postdoctoral Research Fellow in Biology, UT Austin Department of Integrative Bio; Amanda, MA, a client service specialist in a global organization; and Abigail, MD, a Hospitalist at Albany Medical Center. I am indebted to everyone.

Alan T. Belasen

Chapter 1

The Shared Challenge of Middle and Senior Managers

Introduction

Middle managers are an indispensable part of organizational structure and yet their value proposition is hampered by administrative tasks and limited autonomy to fully leverage their strengths or leadership potential. A McKinsey survey (2023) reveals that 43% of middle managers report high burnout, the most across job levels, while 44% cite organizational bureaucracy as a top frustration. In this book, we explore the answers to many questions that relate to interface issues between senior executives and middle managers. Some of these questions include the following.

Why do middle managers report feelings of invisibility (FastCompany, 2024) and under-support, lack of clear communication from the top, and isolation from strategic decision-making? Why are they caught unprepared between the needs of their teams and the expectations of senior leadership

DOI: 10.4324/9781003608028-1

without adequate resources? Do they have the human resources (HR) support and leadership development needed to continue to grow while running daily operations and managing multiple tasks? Do they receive the support and guidance from senior executives to sustain their professional growth? Who, other than middle managers with their cross-hierarchical, cross-boundary roles, can better coordinate complex tasks?

We begin this book by describing the challenges of balancing conflicting priorities and bringing out the best in everyone by leading from the middle out – facilitating and executing business strategies while also considering the needs and concerns of peers and direct reports. We then discuss mitigation strategies that middle managers can use to restore their credibility, overcome stress, and reduce their role conflict.

Senior executives need to understand what motivates middle managers, take steps to improve their decision-making power, and increase their sense of ownership through empowerment and autonomy. Moreover, they should develop the means to include middle managers in dialogic loops, clarify performance metrics and expectations, and help them navigate complex tasks and responsibilities through collaboration and feedback (Belasen & Bertola, 2024). HR directors have a role here, as well – to design targeted leadership development and training programs that strengthen middle managers' leadership, communication, and negotiation skills (Belasen & Frank, 2004).

LEADERSHIP DEVELOPMENT

Three-quarters of 805 HR leaders Gartner surveyed in July 2024 reported **their managers are overwhelmed** by the expansion of their responsibilities, and nearly as many (69%) agreed leaders and managers are not equipped to lead change.

> For organizations to deliver on their goals, managers must be prepared to successfully lead both today and tomorrow…Though 75% of organizations have made significant updates to their leadership development programs, and more than half are increasing spending on leader development, they are not seeing results.
>
> Recent Gartner research revealed that traditional leadership development such as seminars and lectures have a negative effect on development. HR leaders must shift to place more emphasis on intentionally and strategically enabling repeated peer connections for leadership development via networking and team building (Gartner, 2024).

Importantly, this book focuses on bridging the trust gap between senior executives and middle managers for win–win outcomes. Middle managers are best positioned to facilitate implementation of change, engage individuals and teams, and promote the goals of continuous improvement in the workplace. Senior executives can tap into middle managers' functional knowledge and know-how to gain a deeper understanding of operational and resource utilization issues, as well as to gain insights about technical capabilities, benefits, and costs, and evaluate potential risks, allowing for more informed decision-making processes.

Roles and Skills

The Bureau of Labor Statistics (BLS) does not have a single category specifically labeled "middle managers," but instead a broad category of management occupations, which excludes first-line supervisors. This category encompasses various roles, including those often considered middle management like general and operations managers, department managers, and other specialized management roles. These managers oversee the functional areas of the management or administration, such as personnel, purchasing, or administrative services.

Middle managers oversee diverse activities; formulate standard operating procedures (SOPs); manage daily operations; plan, direct, or coordinate resource use; and manage work units through first-line supervisors. They link top executives with frontline leaders, focus on ensuring that tasks are completed efficiently and effectively, and facilitate implementation of strategies within their areas of responsibility.

Financial managers, for example, are responsible for the financial health of an organization. They produce financial reports, direct investment activities, and develop strategies and plans for the long-term financial goals of their organization. Human resources middle managers plan, direct, and coordinate the administrative functions of an organization. They oversee the recruiting, interviewing, and hiring of new staff, consult with top executives on strategic planning, and serve as a link between an organization's management and its employees.

Industrial production managers oversee the daily operations of manufacturing and related plants. They coordinate, plan, and direct the activities used to create a wide range of goods, such as cars, computer equipment, or paper products. In healthcare, middle managers oversee specific departments, such as nursing, surgery, or physical therapy, with responsibilities based on the specialty. Clinical middle managers also set and carry out policies, goals, and procedures for their departments, evaluate the quality of work processes, and write reports and budgets.

The role of the middle manager, however, is evolving with a significant shift toward coaching and empowering individuals and teams rather than solely focusing on supervision and process oversight (Letian, 2023). Middle managers' roles are becoming more fluid and dynamic especially in innovation-driven industries where they unlock the creativity and motivation of frontline employees through synergy, collaborative communication, and trust – the pillars of success (Belasen & Pfeffermann, 2024).

EXTENSIVE ANALYSIS OF JOB POSTINGS

Zhang Letian conducted a unique linguistic analysis of more than 34 million online job postings for managerial openings in the United States between 2007 and 2021. He also gathered and analyzed 1 million newspaper job postings, 6 million manager resumes and job reviews, and 430,000 Indeed.com job reviews.

The data shows the following:

- Managerial job postings that required collaborative skills and experience increased by three times between 2007 and 2021. By contrast, job postings that included supervisory capabilities decreased by 23%.
- The use of collaborative phrases in newspaper job postings grew 15% between 1980 and 2000. Prior to 1980, references to collaboration were scarce.
- The number of managerial resumes listing supervisory experience decreased by 8% between 1985 and 2015, while those highlighting collaboration increased by 37%.
- References to supervisory duties in Indeed.com reviews decreased by 22%, while mentions of collaborative/teamwork skills grew by 28% (Harvard Business School, 2024).

Middle managers act like a vital resource to first-line supervisors and peer managers and are on the lookout for trade-offs that often escape the attention of senior executives and that are essential for the performance of the organization. They use a variety of channels to respond to inquiries from employees, give feedback, and inspire engagement. Knowing what is expected of them and receiving regular feedback on their performance up and down the chain of command is essential for keeping middle managers motivated and engaged.

As change champions, middle managers with active involvement in the strategy process have been found to demonstrate high levels of commitment to organizational goals and contribute to the success of strategic initiatives (Belasen & Luber, 2017). In the healthcare industry, for example, middle managers are an integral part of the organization's resources and capabilities. They support the organization through their know-how, experience, and networking, and help strengthen the social identity and culture of the organization (Belasen & Belasen, 2016).

Furthermore, evidence suggests that middle managers' upward leadership and downward influence appear to affect the alignment of organizational activities within the strategic context. They initiate new ideas to executives and help implement innovation in interactions with lower levels (Belasen & Rufer, 2013).

A variety of management occupations in different organizations (e.g., finance, marketing, technology, engineering) bring with them different cultures and communication practices that must be bridged and mobilized from the middle out for optimal operations. Middle managers make substantial qualitative and quantitative contributions to these organizations, have the know-how to accomplish goals effectively, and provide diverse insights into problem solving.

Middle managers implement strategy, translate goals from top to lower levels, create local relevance, interpret shifting contexts, clarify words and actions of executives, and promote organizational discourse. A sample of their skills and abilities appears in Table 1.1.

Middle managers' central position within the hierarchy facilitates their sensemaking role in interpreting critical events and in creating shared meaning. They balance urgency with consistency by knowing when to provide structure and direction and when to sensibly react to the emotional needs of employees for reliability and clarity. Middle managers' dual lines of managing frontline staff while reporting to senior executives make their roles indispensable during transitions or major disruptions. They search for new opportunities, evaluate the merits of strategic initiatives, and implement innovations

Table 1.1 Skills and Abilities

Compliance	Enable understanding of current regulations and new or proposed policies
Coordination	Facilitate exchanges with executives, peers, and frontline leaders
Tracking	Organize and maintain scheduling and billing information for facilities, suppliers, or distributors
Communication	Support effective communication with supervisors, staff, and external stakeholders
Problem-solving	Provide creative solutions to staffing or other administrative problems
Technology	Stay updated with advances in technology and be familiar with coding and classification software and electronic exchange systems as departments and work units adopt these technologies
Collaboration	Inspire commitment and joint accountability through synergy and teamwork

that move their organizations to new frontiers (Belasen & Belasen, 2017).

Chapters and Topics

This book offers a proven framework of trustworthy leadership along with practical strategies and assessment tools for improving the working relationship between executives and middle managers. Fostering trust and keeping the communication channels open between all levels of management help facilitate a common understanding across hierarchical levels and build the trust needed for achieving desired outcomes.

Chapter 2 – Why Trust Is Important During Times of Disruption

Leadership during disruptive times is not an enviable position to be in. One small decision can change the outcome for better or worse. A wrong move could erode trust and trigger unrest that exacerbates existing conditions.

During uncertain and chaotic times, the need for credible and trustworthy leadership is critical as insecurity can creep in even among most successful executives. Credibility and trustworthiness are a combination of character, expertise, and dependability. Leaders gain credibility when they project compassion and demonstrate that they understand the risks and probable impact of unanticipated consequences. They are aware of their weaknesses and have the humility to defer to experts and delegate responsibilities to competent middle managers.

When executives fail to anticipate disruptions or treat disruptions with less rigor, or when they bypass middle managers rather than engage them in problem-solving, they open themselves up to criticisms. The true test of executive leadership does not occur when everything is running smoothly. It occurs amid unexpected situations when it is crucial to act quickly and communicate sensibly and effectively. Ultimately, senior leadership is about character and doing the right things, acting with moral maturity, using self-control, and valuing input from middle managers.

Trust-based reciprocal relationships enable leaders to serve the people who rely on them, listen to their needs, give praise and recognition, show kindness, display true honesty, and behave authentically. Trust in organizations leads to greater employee engagement, drives higher motivation to work, boosts opportunities for cross-functional collaboration, and promotes learning and development across the organization.

Chapter 3 – The Roles of Middle and Senior Managers in Building Trust

During disruptions, the trust that employees have in their leaders influences the interpretation of insecurity and uncertainty and helps to mitigate employees' perceived threat as they believe in the ability of trustworthy leaders to create safe environments. Leaders whose words and deeds are misaligned will find it challenging to rebuild trust during episodes of disruption.

Trustworthy leaders influence followers through the demonstration of benevolence, high personal integrity, and behavioral tendencies which endure even when the leaders are absent. Leaders need to be sensitive and attuned to moments of difference and feel responsible for working with those differences. They focus on common purposes, are inspirational, and project trustworthiness and empathy that ensure that people stay calm and engaged.

Disruptions can magnify leadership vulnerabilities, particularly how they access, understand, and act upon changing information. Senior executives and middle managers can devise a well-synchronized communication plan that includes responses to early warning signals of a threatening situation and action pathways to deal with the unexpected. Within this context, we explore the critical role of middle managers in managing the tension between these competing commitments and their significant contributions to innovation implementation.

This chapter introduces a framework that establishes the linkage between characteristics of trustworthy leadership and the ability to lead during disruptive times. As it will be pointed out – cultivating attributes of *transparency, accountability, credibility, and honesty* enables organizational leaders to hone the skills needed to be viewed by employees as trustworthy and be prepared for the unexpected (Belasen & Belasen, 2025).

To foster the alignment between actual behaviors and expectations from others, self-assessment can be used periodically to determine how well you have evolved and honed your trustworthy leadership qualities over time. Another option is to obtain feedback from relevant constituents (e.g., stakeholders, executives, board members) using the same survey to assess your perceived trust.

The differences between self-assessment and assessment from others could be very revealing and should lead to a more valid and reliable understanding of potential gaps and how to bridge these gaps. Ideas and actions for improvement or self-development could then be prioritized to reflect inputs from others and eventually lead to a better alignment between the leader's profile on the four dimensions and the perceptions of trustworthiness by others.

An essential part of this chapter also includes insights and practical strategies provided by middle managers who used the assessment instrument as part of their leadership development and self-improvement efforts.

Chapter 4 – Promoting Transparency in the Workplace

Great leaders earn the public trust of followers by communicating with clarity, focus, transparency, and compassion. Without transparency, the public may sense deception, which can reduce the credibility of the leader. In the wake of the COVID-19 pandemic, Singapore's political leadership delivered a series of informative and medically accurate communications and succeeded in conveying clear and trustworthy advice to the public consistent with the best available public health information. The cohesive messaging and understanding that detailed knowledge matters and that the health and economic risks were asymmetrically distributed also facilitated the process of confidence-building, enhanced leadership credibility, and boosted public trust.

A deficiency in transparency occurs when a leader is too inwardly focused, paying disproportionate attention to operational and financial objectives, as well as to managing internal dynamics. While these are important matters and they cannot be ignored, the temptation among many leaders is to act with a sense of urgency rather than strategy. When this occurs, strengths which are assets in regular situations, tend to shift into weaknesses.

Refocusing executive behaviors on transparent communications and using messaging strategies that enhance equity and fairness within the organization and that promote a good alignment of organizational values and stakeholders' views are at the core of trusted leadership.

Chapter 5 – Creating a Culture of Accountability

Accountability reflects the importance of complying with regulations and communicating important decisions or information to key stakeholders. Leaders gain credibility when they project compassion and demonstrate accountability by understanding the risks and probable impact of unanticipated consequences.

Accountability is a construct that involves both an assessment of an individual's beliefs and perceptions of others' beliefs. In self-assessment of accountability, the leaders are accountable to themselves with no presence of others in the decision context. In this case, one would hope that self-accountability also comprises aspects of personal integrity and honesty.

Assessments by others, however, provide added value. When others are involved in assessing the level of leaders' accountability, the leaders (subjects of assessment by others) perceive anyone other than self as evaluating their behavior. Thus, assessments of accountability strengthen the perceived trust between leaders and others.

When leaders experience a deficiency in accountability, it is often marked by a tendency to shoot from the hip, resulting in making authoritative decisions without the benefit of input from affected stakeholders or all the available information. Executives who demonstrate lower levels of accountability need to resist the temptation to make decisions too hastily, even though the urgent pressures of the moment may push them into doing so.

Unless the problem is extremely urgent and a decision must be made on the spot, leaders should reflect before making a choice: Is there information to support the decision? What do we know? What do we not know? How long do we have to decide this? How much time will it take to get the information to validate the issues? Who has the most recent data? Who is involved? What are the risks and costs of ignoring the problem?

Trust is shown when specific mechanisms, (e.g., expectations for accountability) guarantee that those who are trusted behave in the desired manner. Thus, accountability mechanisms function as "protections and inducements" that help manage the risks and rewards when placing trust in an actor. Indeed, caring for followers is one of the outcomes of accountability.

Chapter 6 – Demonstrating Credibility

Credibility and character are perceptions held by others of a person's combination of trustworthiness, expertise, dependability, and empathy. Under different conditions, one or more of those traits may emerge as most important. For leaders tackling disruptions, if any one of the four traits is removed, credibility is likely to suffer. Leaders gain credibility when they project compassion and demonstrate that they understand the risks and probable impact of decisions and actions. They are aware of their weaknesses and have the humility to defer to experts and delegate responsibilities to middle managers.

When leaders and followers are engaged in transparent, honest, accountable, and credible behaviors they also give more attention to self-reflection which can result in effective behavioral change. Leaders who share information about themselves and the organization and who tie ethics and diversity to the long-term success of the organization build a culture of trust with followers and enhance their personal credibility with stakeholders.

Lack of credibility may lead to employee distrust and disengagement adversely affecting the perceptions of leadership competence and trustworthiness as well as the reputation of the organization. Leaders with a deficiency in their credibility often lose their reputation and ability to marshal resources for the common good. They are perceived as political and manipulative and unable to garner sufficient support for their vision, they often resort to making solo decisions. These leaders tend to withhold information and turn to secrecy and closed-door decisions. Credible leaders who lead by example not only are true to themselves but also help others to become more ethical and trusted individuals.

Chapter 7 – Gaining Trust through Honesty

Trusting relationships, especially between executives and middle managers, are developed when the parties perceive each other as having a moral commitment to honesty and truth telling. Honesty is associated with altruistic behavior, positive social relations, unconditional kindness, and reciprocity. Honesty may represent an important antecedent of trustworthiness impressions and trusting behavior across contexts as even small signs of honesty lead people to reciprocate with more trust in future interactions.

A report by *Deloitte Global Human Capital Trends* showed that 80% of business and HR leaders worldwide believed they need to promote leadership capabilities with a focus on openness and honesty as great behavioral mitigators for building trust in organizations. Deficiency in honesty, however, may prove to be the most difficult to remedy, since it relies on the individual's emotional intelligence and the ability to use open communication and empathize with others, especially direct reports.

Creating a culture of honesty and openness that celebrates ethical behavior and publicly acknowledging and rewarding individuals who uphold the highest levels of personal integrity through symbols and action promotes trusting relationships in and around organizations.

Chapter 8 – Bridging the Trust Gap, Finding the Middle Ground

Many middle managers, having reported feelings of being underappreciated, typically point to the lack of information or poor communication from senior executives. Studies show that middle managers operate within the realm of difficult policies, procedures, and guidelines and without a consistent flow of relevant information from the top, are often left unsure of what is required of them. Rarely do we see that commitment to the organization's strategy is problematic for middle managers. Instead, their challenge involves a lack of or untimely communication or limited resources flowing from top executives.

Have middle managers been de-skilled as top executives rationalizing resources and capabilities? Are they secure in their positions? Are they well regarded and targeted for succession planning? Are middle managers well prepared for these challenges? Insufficient middle-manager development could lead to the risk of burnout, disengagement, and high turnover that undermines succession planning. Evidently, higher turnover rates among middle managers might also weaken organizational performance and diminish the vital connection between strategy and execution.

In this chapter, we explore the gap between what executives believe motivates themselves and their middle managers as compared to what middle managers believe motivates themselves and the consequences of mistrust and lack of open communication within the context of this gap. Senior executives are advised to restore trust by enlisting and leveraging the strengths of middle managers to curb the potential for disengagement and the rising costs of middle managers' turnover and replacement.

Chapter 9 – Rebranding Middle Managers

This chapter concludes the book with leadership assessment and development. It encourages executives and middle managers to undertake a journey of self-assessment to discover their strengths and weaknesses while being true to themselves and others. It is about knowing yourself.

Self-aware leaders reflect on their personal strengths and weaknesses, are sensitive to how others perceive their words and actions, and act on feedback to take corrective steps to remedy their weaknesses so trustworthiness can be preserved. Self-awareness leads to personal control and growth that helps leaders play to their personal strengths in guiding individuals and teams to pursue targeted outcomes.

Trustworthy leaders project credibility and honesty by prioritizing organizational needs above their own and by creating a safe and inclusive environment where organizational members feel valued and respected. They foster transparent communications and demonstrate personal accountability by reflecting on inputs from others and by following through to see things to the end.

Conclusion

Each chapter in this book is more than a collection of ideas. Furthermore, each chapter is a part of a trustworthy leadership framework with four important dimensions – transparency, honesty, credibility, and accountability – that encompass traits, skills, behaviors, and qualities of how and why senior executives and middle managers must trust each other.

Building trust is a vital condition for achieving a "win–win" outcome because when senior executives and middle managers trust each other, they are more likely to openly communicate, collaborate, and find integrative solutions that benefit the entire organization. *Transparent Leadership* fosters a cooperative environment where mutual benefit is prioritized and shared success is the glue that bonds everyone together.

References

Belasen, A. & Pfeffermann, N. (2024). *Brilliant Leadership – Unlocking the Power of Innovation-Communication,* New York, NY: Routledge.

Belasen, A. T. & Belasen, A. R. (2016). Value in the Middle: Cultivating Middle Managers in Healthcare Organizations, *Journal of Management Development,* 35(9), 1149–1162.

Belasen, A. T. & Belasen, A. R. (2017). Strengthening the Middle Line: Overcoming Motivational Gaps, Supporting Promising Managers, Best Paper, *Proceedings of the Seventy-Seventh Annual Meeting of the Academy of Management.* Online ISSN: 2151-6561. https://doi.org/10.5465/AMBPP.2017.7

Belasen, A. T. & Belasen, A. R. (2025). Signaling Trust During Disruptions: Perceived Gender Differences in Trustworthy Leadership Traits, *Gender in Management: An International Journal.* https://doi.org/10.1108/GM-04-2024-0187.

Belasen, A. T. & Bertola, L. (2024). Co-Creation, Strategic Visioning, and Iterative Loops. In Alan T Belasen & Nicole Pfeffermann (Eds.), *Brilliant Leadership – Unlocking the Power of Innovation-Communication,* pp. 63–77, New York, NY: Routledge.

Belasen, A. & Frank, N. M. (2004). The Perceptions of Human Resource Managers of the Shifting Importance of Managerial Roles in Downsizing Organizations, *International Journal of Human Resources Development and Management*, 4(2), 144–163.

Belasen, A. & Luber, E. (2017). Innovation Implementation: Leading from the Middle Out. In Nicole Pfeffermann & Julie Gould (Eds.), *Strategy and Communication for Innovation: Integrative Perspectives on Innovation in the Digital Economy*, pp. 229–243, Germany: Springer.

Belasen, A. & Rufer, R. (2013). Innovation Communication for Effective Inter-professional Collaboration: A Stakeholder Perspective. In Nicole Pfeffermann, Tim Minshall, & Letizia Mortara (Eds.), *Strategy and Communication for Innovation*, 2nd edition, pp. 227–240, Germany: Springer.

FastCompany. (2024). 82% of Middle Managers Feel Invisible—Here's Why, November 22, https://www.fastcompany.com/91231972/82-of-middle-managers-feel-invisible-heres-why.

Gartner. (2024). Gartner Survey Finds Leader and Manager Development Tops HR Leaders' List of 2025 Priorities for Third Consecutive Year, October 15, https://www.gartner.com/en/newsroom/press-releases/2024-10-15-gartner-survey-finds-leader-and-manager-development-tops-hrleaders-list#:~:text=Three%2Dquarters%20of%20805%20HR,not%20equipped%20to%20lead%20change.

Harvard Business School.(2024). The Middle Manager of the Future: More Coaching, Less Commanding, *Working Knowledge*, February 5, https://www.library.hbs.edu/working-knowledge/the-middle-manager-of-the-future-more-coaching-less-commanding.

Letian, Z (2023). The Changing Role of Managers, *American Journal of Sociology*, 129(2), 439–484.

McKinsey. (2023). Stop Wasting your Most Precious Resource: Middle Managers, https://www.mckinsey.com/capabilities/people-and-organizational-performance/our-insights/stop-wasting-your-most-precious-resource-middle-managers.

Chapter 2

Why Trust Is Important During Times of Disruption

Introduction

Developing and preserving trust in organizations is vital for success on two fronts – internally and externally. Internally, trust is the foundation of teamwork and enhanced collaboration, creating strong interpersonal relationships and establishing a culture of safety and reliability. Within the organization, employees can explore and share new ideas, they feel respected by their leaders, and confident in their interactions, leading to higher loyalty and retention.

Externally, trust is vital for building credibility with suppliers and customers, as it enables transparent communication in problem-solving and risk mitigation between partners across the value chain, ensuring the delivery of reliable products and services and a strong reputation for the entire chain.

This chapter covers trust in and around organizations – the level of confidence employees, customers, suppliers, and

DOI: 10.4324/9781003608028-2

other stakeholders have in the leadership, goals, strategies, and executive decisions, encompassing not just internal relationships among employees and their managers, but also the perceived credibility of the organization by external audiences. The sections in this chapter focus on the internal and external dynamics that enable trustworthiness – the degree to which employees and stakeholders expect the organization to act consistently with integrity and reliability across diverse contexts, especially during disruptions.

Building Trust

Trust is built through confidence and is demonstrated in the leader's attitudes, skills, and abilities, and followers' acceptance of the leader's direction and vision. It generates increased employee engagement, better team performance, and higher levels of personal and organizational productivity. Trustworthy leaders empower employees to take ownership of their roles and responsibilities. Employees feel secure and supported, enabling them to take calculated risks, share new ideas, and explore creative solutions to challenges.

When individuals trust that their decisions and actions are valued and significantly contribute to the organization, they feel a sense of enablement and purpose. Enabled employees are more engaged and proactive, more willing to embrace and appreciate each other, and more willing to collaborate and maintain a sense of collective resilience in the face of disruption.

Trust is the foundation of identity in as far as it influences the interactions between employees and managers, builds relationships, and shapes how individuals perceive themselves. But it is also a strategic differentiator in the marketplace. Trust that is aligned with the goals of sustainability fosters added loyalty by conscious customers, partners, and stakeholders, giving the organization a unique advantage in the market. When trust turns into loyalty, external audiences are more likely to support the decisions, actions, and outcomes, allowing the brand to differentiate itself from the competition by highlighting its practices and set of commitments.

Disruption

Anticipating industry disruptions and capitalizing on emerging trends is critical for gaining competitive advantage over rival organizations. Disruptions may include talent gaps and labor shortages affecting industry productivity or innovation implementation, but also supplier delays or logistical failures, natural disasters (e.g., droughts, earthquakes, floods, heat waves) impacting operations, IT outages or equipment breakdowns, unanticipated shifts in consumer preferences, entry of new competitors, technological overhauls, regulatory shifts, and economic downturns.

Organizational level disruptions include long-standing problems, inefficiencies, outdated products, or service pain points, potentially causing significant shifts in the market dynamics and requiring established companies to adapt or potentially face erosion in their market share and ultimately a decline.

PRIORITIZING CUSTOMERS

Technology itself is not the prime disruptor in today's landscape. More traditional businesses that have been slow to embrace customer-centric thinking are the ones rendered most vulnerable to disruption. Any company that remains complacent by prioritizing legacy practices over evolving customer needs is at risk of being left behind.

The greatest threat facing businesses of all sizes and industries is not emerging technologies per se. It's the failure to relentlessly cultivate a customer obsession and culture of empathy throughout the organization. Those that have mastered putting the customer first and radically rethinking service delivery through their customer's lens are positioned to thrive – whether as upstarts or innovators from within (Kennedy, 2024).

Leadership during disruptive times is not an enviable position to be in. One small decision can change the outcome for the better or worse. Even a seemingly insignificant choice executives make may be susceptible to a substantial impact on outcomes, leading to nonlinear consequences, illustrating the concept of the "butterfly effect" where minor decisions can create large ripple effects (Lorenz, 1963).

A wrong move could erode trust or trigger instability that exacerbates current or new conditions in and around the organization. Inspiring employees and regaining their trust during disruptions require a combination of character, expertise, and dependability. When leaders and employees are confident in each other's intentions and actions, it creates opportunities for an open, collaborative, and productive work environment in which everyone feels comfortable in sharing ideas and supporting one another.

HUMANS AND MACHINES – PERFECT PARTNERS FOR MARKETING'S NONLINEARITY

We now accept the uncertainty of weather. As Edward Lorenz discovered, analytic systems make excellent partners to help humans with important tasks necessary to thrive in a complex world. A quick look at the weather app on your phone predicts the possibility of rain two weeks out. During volatile seasons, we check the app more frequently to keep on top of change. We have more insight into weather now, but we still understand that as we move out in time, the picture gets murkier.

Executives must adopt a similar mindset for markets. Accept marketing will never be a machine. All the data in the world will not tame nonlinearity. Gain competence in working with probabilities. Think like an investor. Evaluate returns on marketing programs within the context of the ever-changing market. Use metrics as directional tools to answer the question "are we headed towards where we want to go?" Hold objectives loosely and be ready to pivot (Schaub, 2023).

Building trust and confidence in the workplace enables employees to become deeply invested in the company's brand image, take ownership of their tasks and responsibilities, and actively strive to fulfill promises made to customers and stakeholders. This also helps leaders shape a compelling vision for the future, strengthen their perceived trustworthiness, and heighten the brand image and reputation of the organization.

Reputation

Reputation building is the process of creating a positive image and gaining trust with others. A reputation develops from the uniqueness of the organization's culture, core values, and leadership characteristics. Importantly, it is sustained through enduring identity-shaping practices and commitments that get the public to perceive the organization as reliable and trustworthy. Over time, it fosters the view that the organization is highly reputable and that its leaders and employees exhibit high levels of empathy and personal integrity in their communications and behaviors. As an example, Apple's core values of diversity, equity, sustainability, and supplier responsibility significantly contributed to the company's reputation among consumers and stakeholders alike.

Reputation is translated into building credibility with stakeholders and customers by taking concrete steps to address their concerns and by following through with delivery of reliable products and services. E-commerce platforms like Amazon revolutionized retail by offering a sizable virtual marketplace with fast and flexible delivery options, impacting traditional retailers that rely on store traffic and low inventory rather than on speed and variety.

JEFF BEZOS ON HIS 4-STEP METHOD FOR BUILDING TRUST AND REPUTATION

In 2019, Bezos laid out the four things he does to earn people's trust:

1. **Do hard things**

"The way you earn trust, the way you develop a reputation," Bezos said, "is by doing hard things well over and over again."

Bezos uses the US military as an example. Although the American public's trust and confidence in the military has fallen since 2018, it remains one of the most trusted institutions in the country "by a large margin," according to the Reagan Presidential Foundation and Institute.

"The reason that the military has such high credibility and reputation is because, over and over again, decade after decade, it has done hard things well."

2. **If you say you're going to do something, do it**

"It really is that simple. It's also that complicated," Bezos said. "Because to do hard things well, you must have integrity and competence. That means doing what you said you were going to do — and delivering."

Amazon, he said, delivers more than a billion packages a year: "We say we're going to do that, and then we actually do it."

3. **Take controversial stances**

While one could argue that people who are agreeable tend to be trustworthy and have good intentions, Bezos doesn't believe that's always the case.

"People like it when you say, 'No, we're not going to do it that way. I know you want us to do it that way, but we're not going to,' the Amazon founder said. "And even if they disagree, they might say, 'We kind of respect that, though'. They know who they are."

4. **Have clarity**

When taking controversial stances, Bezos says it's helpful to have clarity.

"If we are clear that we're going to do this and we aren't going to do that, then people can opt in or out," he explained. "They can say, 'Well, if that's Amazon's position or Blue Origin's position on something, then I don't want to be part of that."

And that's something Bezos is okay with.

"We live in a big democracy with lots of opinions," he added. "I want to live in a place where people can disagree and can still work together. I don't want to lose that. People are entitled to their opinions, but it is the job of a senior leadership team to say no" (Popomaronis, 2021).

Identity and Image

Corporate identity reflects the internal values, culture, and self-perception of a company while corporate image is the interpretation of a company's core values and beliefs which are formed in the minds of multiple stakeholders and customers. A brand image mirrors how a company wants its target audience to perceive it, focusing on stakeholder relationship and customer experience.

How organizational members view themselves internally largely affects how the public (i.e., stakeholders, customers) views the organization over time. Both work in tandem to create a brand's reputation, credibility, and recognition. Thus, aligning corporate identity with brand image, the visual representation of a product or service that shapes the company's presence in the marketplace, plays a vital role in the confidence that customers and stakeholders have in the ability of the company to deliver on commitments reliably.

Strong identity evolves into an ideology that enables the organization to bond itself internally and induce members to support the vision of the organization. Fittingly, a successful brand image yields positive results and ultimately becomes a powerful tool for distinguishing the organization from its competitors.

When image and identity are aligned across digital platforms and communication channels, the organization is externally adaptive and internally cohesive. When the external image and internal identity are misaligned (i.e., they are not presenting themselves in a way that aligns with their intended perception), stakeholders may become confused, and the credibility of the organization may erode (Sanders, Bertola, & Belasen, 2024).

Shaping and sustaining the image of the organization is therefore a strategic imperative that requires a broad understanding of internal and external dynamics. It gets executives and middle managers to act as if they are paranoid communicators – constantly scanning the external environment and sorting through the multiple images that are formed by diverse stakeholders.

The goal is to address possible vulnerabilities and realign the corporate identity and message strategies, brand values, and customer experiences across all touchpoints. This ensures that the communications, core beliefs, and interactions with external audiences reflect the corporate image authentically, regardless of where or how (online or onsite) stakeholders or customers engage with the brand.

Trust and Customer Loyalty

Building trust is a strategic differentiator that drives business growth through enhanced stakeholder confidence and unique market positioning. Trust is a key factor in developing and sustaining customer loyalty, especially during disruptions when customers look up to the company's ability to provide reliable services. Integrating trust-building strategies into core business operations creates a deeper bond between the organization and its customers and drives higher levels of loyalty and retention.

Trust that draws on consistent messaging, quality products, and positive customer experiences, also contributes to the credibility of the brand image by motivating customers to repeatedly choose that brand over rivals, further cultivating customer loyalty. A positive brand image mediated by high perceived quality leads to greater brand loyalty, as consumers trust that the brand will consistently meet their expectations even during disruptions. This mediation process strengthens loyalty through brand identity, repeated purchases, and continued consumer satisfaction (García-Salirrosas et al., 2024).

Integrating loyalty within a business strategy can significantly drive growth and profitability by encouraging repeat purchases and by building and retaining a more stable customer base (Alemany, 2024). Therefore, cultivating long-term, dedicated customer relationships is not only an internal asset but also a strategic differentiator. It allows the brand to stand out and the company to sustain its competitive advantage even when faced with significant market disruptions. This is done through a customer-centric business model that prioritizes innovation and adaptability and consistently delivers exceptional service while pursuing customer feedback and creating personalized experiences that bond customers emotionally with the brand.

A prime example of a company with strong customer loyalty and emotional connection that aligns the brand with the company's core values is Apple. With its feedback-driven, transparent communication, and customer-centric approach which prioritizes user experience, Apple has built long-term relationships with customers. These loyal customers repeatedly choose Apple over competitors' products, recommend them to others, and remain loyal even when faced with price fluctuations or new options in the marketplace. This fierce loyalty is fueled by the trust customers have in Apple's leadership's unwavering commitment to innovation and quality.

Tim Cook, Apple's CEO, is known for his collaborative leadership style and strong focus on integrity, ethical business practices, and social justice initiatives. Tim Cook's leadership, which prioritizes sustainable growth and long-term value combined has continued to shape further the trust and loyalty developed over time with Apple's employees, investors, and the public.

Golden Circle

Simon Sinek's (2011) Golden Circle is an actionable leadership roadmap consisting of three components: Why, How, and What. Great leaders recognize "why" customers need what their organization offers, then move on to focus on "how" their organization's key performance metrics and non-imitated operational effectiveness distinguish them from industry rivals and finally share the details of their products and services – the "what."

Starting with "why" when communicating the strategy, leaders highlight the impact or difference an organization aims to make – social, technological, environmental, economic, or a blend of these factors – through activities and services in its target area, and why it matters. Internally, this inspires teams and employees to own the common purpose and commit to meaningful actions. Externally, the "why" taps into followers' brains (subliminally) and influences behavior, making it a powerful means for inspiring and retaining customers and stakeholders.

The "how" in the Golden Circle requires knowledgeable middle managers and professionals familiar with industry pain points where customers or businesses face significant challenges or frustrations. They provide innovative solutions that address these pain points, often by leveraging analytic capabilities and emerging technologies. These solutions provide access to a wider range of customers, by lowering costs or simplifying the user's experience.

Apple's rise to fame is attributed to the articulation of its "why" – to disrupt the existing industry by promoting divergent thinking and innovative ideas and solutions that fundamentally change the way the industry operates. Apple's "why" primarily focuses on the mission to enrich people's daily experiences by making technology intuitive and accessible through innovative design and seamless integration across high quality devices. Indeed, this innovative design goes beyond the operating system, hardware, and user interface.

Apple's design philosophy prioritizes user-centric experience, simplicity, and elegance, which drives every action, setting Apple apart from its competitors. It aligns the "how" with the "why" by creating attractive products, including the iPhone, which appeals to customers with their aesthetic style and user-friendly interface.

Apple's "what" represents the products and services Apple offers, which result from its "why." Thus, Apple's processes, operating procedures, workflow (how), and products (what) align with the company's "why" (core values) for consistency and authenticity.

Inspiring Action

According to Sinek (2011), great leaders inspire action by harnessing the power of *WHY, e*mbracing and communicating the purpose behind their decisions and actions. "Why" is the organization's value proposition that differentiates it from competitors and builds credibility with stakeholders who share the values of the organization. Articulating the "why" motivates individuals and teams to commit to the long-term goals and vision. It drives success by encouraging trust, collaboration, and transformation.

Leading by example: Modeling high integrity, self-awareness, and empathy for the entire organization. Integrity is the foundation of trustworthy leadership, which involves transparency, accountability, and honesty. Trustworthy leaders "walk their talk" by playing to strengths while admitting weaknesses and improving by learning from failure. Self-aware leaders continuously use empathy to understand and engage others, value input from diverse teams, and develop meaningful relationships.

Encouraging innovation and growth: Challenging the status quo and promoting an innovative culture that drives an adaptive mindset in the workplace. A culture of innovation encourages creativity, exploration, and a willingness to embrace change, where employees are empowered to learn, adapt, and continuously look for new ideas to respond effectively to evolving market conditions, and where high tolerance for failure is used as an opportunity for personal and professional growth.

Trustworthy leaders urge team members to question core assumptions, challenge existing rules, beliefs, or practices to identify gaps and implement new ideas and approaches. This approach enables organizations to embody a growth mindset, encourage appropriate risk-taking behaviors, evolve, adapt, and ensure the organization's value proposition remains salient.

The Disruptor's Advantage

Industry disruptors embrace a culture of experimentation by trying new ideas quickly, failing fast in the early stages of testing new ideas, and learning from mistakes to rapidly assess what works and what does not work. They then use that knowledge to pivot and develop more successful innovations, further accelerating the overall innovation process. Other characteristics include agility, collaboration, adaptation, and a customer-centric mindset that put the customer's needs and preferences front and center; data analytics to identify trends, expected outcomes, and actions to improve performance; and a persistent focus on disrupting existing markets by offering new, convenient, and often inexpensive solutions.

Disruptive cultures are passionate about their customers. They focus on designing and developing new products, services, or experiences by actively considering the needs, wants, and pain points of customers throughout the entire innovation process, ensuring that the final solution directly addresses their problems and provides real value to their customers. The culture of industry disruptors like Netflix, Uber, and Amazon is commonly characterized by a strong customer-centric innovation which prioritizes divergent thinking, creativity, exploration, risk-taking and a persistent effort to scan the business environment, adapt to emerging market demands, and monitor competitors' efforts (Belasen & Bertola, 2024).

Netflix offers innovative products and services by leveraging user data to personalize recommendations, and experiments with new streaming formats by constantly evolving and pushing boundaries. It relies on data analytics to inform strategy, product development, and marketing decisions and employs flexible work processes to respond swiftly to changing consumer needs and preferences.

Amazon prioritizes speed of delivery, offering a vast product selection, while constantly innovating its logistics and cloud computing services. Uber uses ride-sharing apps that disrupt the taxi industry by providing a more convenient and accessible way to book rides through a mobile app, focusing on user experience, and adapting to local regulations to expand market reach.

UBER'S COLLABORATIVE LEADERSHIP TO EMPLOYEE EMPOWERMENT

Khosrowshahi believes in building a culture where employees are trusted to take ownership of their work. Furthermore, his approach includes decentralizing decision-making, allowing different units within Uber to operate independently and swiftly. As a result, this autonomy helps maintain agility and innovation within the company, even as it grows larger. He emphasizes that Uber's Collaborative Leadership, which empowers employees with responsibility and freedom, is key to maintaining a high-performance culture.

He also invests in employee development through mentorship programs and leadership training. In addition, these initiatives not only foster talent but also help align the workforce with Uber's long-term goals. Regular communication, such as town hall meetings, encourages transparency and ensures that employees feel heard and valued, ultimately contributing to a more inclusive and engaged work environment.

Under Khosrowshahi's leadership, Uber has made significant strides in promoting diversity and inclusion. He has implemented recruitment strategies aimed at increasing the representation of underrepresented groups and has fostered a corporate culture that values diverse perspectives. This focus on inclusion is not just about ethics but also about driving innovation and global growth goals (Alshareef, 2024).

Building a Culture of Trust

Prioritizing trust-building behaviors and modeling trustworthy leadership practices, upholding ethical values, and ensuring that these values and practices transcend organizational lines are key for building a culture of trust and sustaining long-term branding strategy.

A culture of trust helps bond organizational members internally and sends a strong message to external audiences about a cohesive corporate brand that aligns individual goals and actions with a common purpose and commitment to attain strategic objectives.

Building a culture of trust permeates all levels of the organization and creates a working environment in which employees and managers feel psychologically safe to express their opinions or concerns, communicate openly with peers without worrying about spillover and crossover effects of incivility like harsh criticism, retribution, or job insecurity. These employees are rewarded for taking calculated risks that move them outside their comfort zone and that expand their "sweet spot" for developing new skills and promoting continuous learning.

Streaming services like Netflix disrupt the traditional way people watch movies and episodic television by offering on-demand access to a wide offering, disrupting the traditional video rental market. Netflix attracts and retains exceptional talent to design the best products at scale by focusing on creativity, critical thinking, and entrepreneurial spirit. Employees at Netflix have permission to innovate, propose ideas, and take risks by learning from failure to rapidly improve customer experience.

Being Trustworthy

During uncertain and chaotic times, the need for credible and trustworthy leadership is critical as insecurity can creep in on even the most successful executive. Prioritizing trust-building behaviors and modeling trustworthy leadership practices, upholding ethical values, and ensuring that these values and practices permeate organizational lines and work units are key for building a culture of trust and for sustaining long-term branding strategy. Trustworthy leaders who foster a positive work environment and who believe in their employees' potential are more likely to have a workforce motivated to overcome disruptions and achieve success.

Leaders gain credibility when they project compassion and demonstrate that they understand the risks and probable impact of decisions. They are aware of their weaknesses and have the humility to defer judgment to experts and delegate responsibilities to middle managers with the know-how to facilitate change and maintain long-term achievements. Trustworthy leaders who focus on anticipating potential problems or obstacles before they arise and take steps to lessen their impact, also foster trust and confidence in their abilities to address even the most extreme challenges.

TRUST – THE ULTIMATE DIFFERENTIATOR

The absence of trust can have detrimental consequences. A lack of trust breeds fear, suspicion, and internal competition, hindering collaboration and stifling creativity. Employees become guarded and reluctant to share ideas or feedback, leading to a siloed working environment that obstructs problem-solving and hinders progress. Ultimately, this affects the quality of products or services delivered to customers.

It is essential to recognize that trust cannot be built solely through the efforts of individual team members. It must be modeled and championed by the executive leadership. Leaders play a crucial role in establishing and reinforcing trust. When leaders are transparent, honest, and consistent in their actions and decisions, it sets the tone for the entire organization. Trust cascades from the top down, creating a culture of trust that permeates through all levels of the organization.

Building trust is not a one-time event; it requires continuous effort and dedication. Organizations must continually leverage strategies that promote trust to maintain a positive and cohesive work environment. These strategies can include fostering open communication, providing opportunities for team-building activities, recognizing and rewarding trust-building behaviors, and offering channels for feedback and suggestions (Hunt, 2023).

When executives fail to think and act responsibly or when they bypass middle managers for sources of information, rely on defensive communications, or treat disruptions with less rigor, they open themselves up to social media activism and public criticism. The true test of executive leadership does not occur when everything is running smoothly. It occurs amid unexpected situations when it is crucial to act quickly and communicate sensibly and effectively.

Ultimately, leadership is about character and doing the right thing, acting with personal integrity, having self-control, and valuing input from middle managers. Demonstrating unassuming behavior is another critical aspect of trust-building in leader–follower relationships.

Leaders who reveal their weaknesses demonstrate that they are approachable and create a workplace where trusting relationships can thrive, encouraging others to be more engaged and committed. Admitting vulnerabilities through self-disclosure can be a powerful medium for projecting authenticity because it demonstrates a genuine willingness to be open and honest about one's limitations. When leaders begin with self-understanding, disclose their strengths and weaknesses, and identify how others perceive them, they are viewed as less arrogant and more approachable as well as get a sense of validation about potential gaps that need to be bridged. This helps increase their perceived trustworthiness by followers. Research shows that authentic leadership reinforces employees' emotional connection with their organizations and promotes better on-the-job performance (Duarte et al., 2021).

Being recognized as trustworthy enables leaders to serve the people that rely on them, listen to their needs, give praise and recognition, show kindness, display true honesty and behave authentically. Trust in organizations leads to greater employee engagement, drives higher motivation to work, boosts opportunities for cross-functional collaboration, and promotes learning and development across the organization.

Reciprocal Trust

Establishing a common understanding and clarifying mutually serving intentions are powerful means for building trust in organizations. Reciprocal trust in which employees and their leaders mutually trust each other encourages employees to take calculated risks when fulfilling their roles, using creativity, and prioritizing flexibility in strategy development or innovation implementation. Externally, it creates opportunities for growth and venturing into new markets, actively seeking out and implementing new approaches, adopting innovative strategies, testing cutting-edge technologies, and creating significantly new and impactful products or services. These levers could potentially disrupt the market or challenge the established industry norms, forcing competitors to adapt or potentially lose market share.

Reciprocal trust is not a one-time event; it requires mutual efforts by leaders and employees toward building a positive work climate. Studies show that the negative relationship between isolation and trust is primarily established by reduced organizational communication quality and interpersonal information-sharing quality compared to the frequency of communication (Van Zoonen, Sivunen, & Blomqvist, 2024). Leaders play a crucial role in establishing reciprocal trust through open communication. When leaders are transparent and honest in their communications, they project trustworthiness that cascades from the top down and that builds confidence in their ability to preserve organizational trust during disruption (Belasen & Belasen, 2025).

WHAT IS LEADERSHIP TRUST?

Trust means "uncompromised by doubt." In the workplace, people can't do their best work if they doubt others' intentions or capabilities, the direction or viability of the organization, or, most importantly, their own ability to keep up with the demands placed on them. This is especially true in today's environment of complex change and ambiguity, when employees are being asked to do more with less.

Leadership trust is reciprocal and created incrementally. To inspire trust from others, leaders need to also show trust in them. Over time these relationships build and maintain trust that teams and organizations need to act in a fast-paced world.

Our research underscores the need for trust in organizations. In high-trust environments, people show up and do their best work. They gain productive energy, creativity, speed, and better results. They align around a common purpose, take risks, support each other, and communicate openly and honestly.

Effective leadership requires knowing how to build and keep trust, whether it is with individuals, on teams, or across the organization (Reina & Reina, 2024).

Leadership is a process of influence and is context specific. It cannot occur without followers who willingly accept and comprehend the direction and vision of the leader. Leaders must clearly communicate their vision, goals, and expectations to gain follower consent. At the same time, followers need to trust leaders' aspirations and abilities to willingly follow them even in their absence.

Leadership is not bound by the traditional superior–subordinate relationship. It can emerge anywhere in the organization. Employees follow their leaders because they offer valuable insights, expertise, or a unique perspective that engages and inspires them to trust the leaders' judgment. When a leader demonstrates authenticity and trustworthiness, consistently respects followers' inputs and continuously communicates timely messages that are relevant and useful, they feel valued and connected emotionally to the leader (Belasen & Bertola, 2024).

When followers identify their values with the values of the leader who provide something meaningful that they cannot easily find elsewhere, they become more engaged and supportive of the leader's endeavors. In turn, the leader's ability to influence their followers' attitudes and behaviors becomes a source of referent power. Followers accept the leader's directions through emotional attachment and admiration that are sustained through reciprocal relationships and emulation.

Some scholars have suggested that leader–follower exchanges are more reciprocal and mutually beneficial when they are more symmetrical (i.e., have more equal social bargaining power). However, as followers rely more frequently on leaders whose high status becomes less dependent on their willingness to pay the costs of benefitting followers, service-for-prestige theory predicts that leader–follower relations will become based more on the leaders' ability to dominate and exploit rather than benefit the followers (Price & Van Vugt, 2014).

We contend, however, that authentic leaders who gain the trust of followers and who demonstrate the values of trustworthiness and personal integrity are likely to become good role models and be imitated by followers. Authentic leaders can effectively drive follower identification, fostering beneficial outcomes. These leaders are respectful of followers' views and suggestions, are open minded and receptive to new ideas, show appreciation for followers' accomplishments, and inspire them to be productive members of the organization.

When referent power (i.e., the ability to influence others based on identification) is used by authentic leaders responsibly and ethically to create a safe environment with open exchanges of ideas and solutions, it helps leaders attract, reward, and retain talent and, at the same time, preserve reciprocal trust in the organization. Authentic leaders facilitate a sense of belonging to the organization, inspire followers' identification with the mission and goals of the organization, encourage transparency, set clear lines of accountability, and actively support the development of followers' skills and abilities (Jun, Hu, & Lee, 2023).

Moreover, since transformational and authentic forms of leadership overlap, authentic leaders are likely to stimulate follower's personal identification with them by setting positive examples, such as displaying high moral standards, honesty, and integrity. Leadership behaviors of this nature facilitate a strong bond between followers and their leaders, resulting in a gradual alignment of their respective values, beliefs, goals, and actions (Avolio et al., 2004).

Hence, reciprocal forms of trust where leaders and followers feel empowered to contribute freely and take risks without fear of repercussion are critical for building trusting relationships and cohesive teams. Reciprocal trust fosters open communication, increases employee engagement, and ultimately helps to achieve organizational success. It requires collaborative forms of leadership with complementary roles.

Complementary Roles

There is no question that both leadership and management are vital to the successful operation of organizations. But management and leadership have different centralities: Management is job-centered, whereas leadership is employee centered. Management is responsible for the attainment of operational plans and goals. Managers use centralized authority for controlling and directing the behavior of employees to ensure stability and reliability on organizational operations. In management, the executive serves an operational role, having control over resource allocation and responsibility for the outcome of the employees' actions.

Leadership, on the other hand, is not bound by the hierarchical relations that govern administrative positions. Rather, leadership is a process of influence that shapes the identity of followers through persuasion and inspiration. This follows Barro's (1973) theory of the Principal–Agent model. Managers present an "Agency Cost" to shareholders because their interests do not necessarily align with the profit-seeking interests of the shareholders. This is because executives cannot perfectly monitor managers, leading to the risk that managers may act on their own interests for self-promotion rather than those of the shareholder.

Good management maintains stability, predictability, and order through a desired *culture of efficiency*; leadership creates change within a *culture of integrity* that helps the organization thrive over the long term by promoting openness and honesty, positive relationships, and long-term innovation. Leadership cannot replace management; it can only complement it.

Although "manager" and "leader" are typically considered contrasting roles, and as leadership is not bound by position, in theory anyone in an organization can have a leadership presence, including a manager. Moreover, because of the fluidity of many forms of organizational structure, managers are often leaders and leaders are often managers. The term "manager" indicates a transactional, authoritative position derived from the organizational hierarchy that is concerned with internal consistency, procedures and policies, setting goals for employees, and emphasizing tasks and duties.

Conversely, a leader interacts with others to create a shared purpose and reality, helping followers to identify with the brand. Leaders exhibit behaviors and intentions that communicate the mission and vision of the organization, examine new perspectives and creative ideas for solving problems, and nurture the leadership pipeline. In fact, for an organization to succeed, leadership and management must go hand in hand. The challenge for success lies in balancing management duties with leadership utilities – the attributes of balanced leaders.

The key to sustaining balanced leadership is to capably integrate elements of management with qualities of leadership (Figure 2.1) and use a situational approach to flexibly tailor the appropriate role to the task or individual needs. Leadership greatness is gauging the appropriate timing and course of their actions – knowing intuitively when to relinquish control and empower others to take the lead (A), and when to act alone at the forefront of the decision-making process (B). Balanced leaders have the unique talent to recognize situations at critical conjunctures and use the right balance of roles to achieve desired objectives.

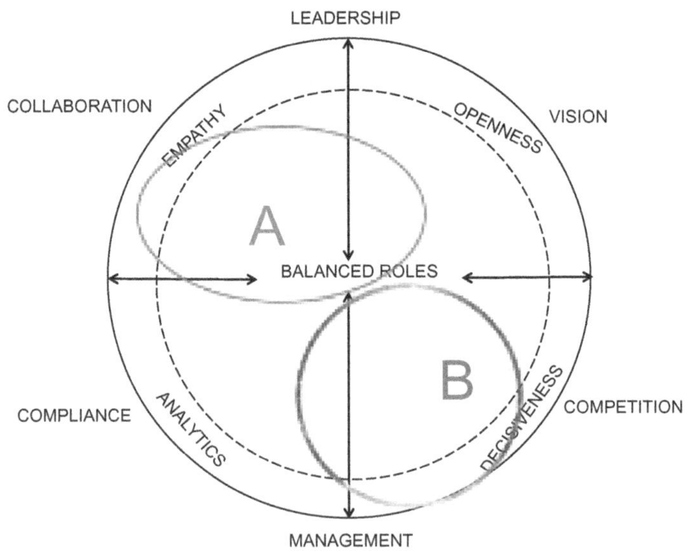

Figure 2.1 Balanced Roles

Rather than arbitrarily adopting a single style that falls within the leader's "comfort zone" of skills and attitudes, balanced leaders recognize the value of adapting to diverse situations and contexts. They harmonize seemingly opposing qualities like compliance, decisiveness, and short-term goals (management) with empathy, collaboration, and long-term vision (leadership). Such a leadership mode enables leaders to operate within the "sweet spot" – to move forward with plans and goals while considering the well-being of team members.

Complex tasks require leaders to display assertiveness, much needed for critical decisions. However, they also rely on strong emotional intelligence skills to build consensus during emergent (and often unknown) situations. In this context, trust plays a vital role as the foundation upon which a leader can successfully rebalance these diverse, seemingly exclusive roles, and preserve the "sweet spot."

Trust is the glue which binds followers and their leaders during disruptive times. Balanced leaders with behavioral flexibility focus on the common purpose, are competent, inspirational, and trustworthy and ensure people remain focused and engaged. The ability to balance abstract thinking with confidence, agility with attention to details, and decisiveness with empathy allows these leaders to navigate challenging events successfully. Confident leaders project success through optimism and trust and with their ability to guide people and overcome challenges.

Such leaders are effective in achieving positive and enduring outcomes even when their organizations are tested, especially during disruptions when followers rely heavily on leaders to provide direction, reassurance, and updates. Evidence from the 2021 *Edelman Trust Barometer* at the time that overlapped with the COVID-19 pandemic corroborated this. The survey revealed that "people don't know where or who to turn to for reliable information." A majority of respondents believed that government leaders (57%) and media

(59%) are purposely trying to mislead people by quoting false facts. Business leaders and their companies, however, emerged as the most trustworthy institutions (61%), replacing government (53%) and outscoring government by 48% on competency. Trustworthiness has continued to move in a local direction, with respondents placing even higher ratings on "my employer" at 76%, and "my employer CEO" at 63%.

Conclusion

Internally, trust is the key to creating a safe environment where healthy relationships, realization of innovation, and employee engagement can thrive. Building a culture of trust improves work motivation, reduces turnover, and increases higher productivity. By prioritizing trust-building strategies and modeling trustworthiness from the top, organizations can position themselves for long-term success.

Externally, building credibility in the value chain through trusting relationships is regarded as fundamental towards effectively establishing collaboration in supply chains and has been found to be a key reason behind the success of the interdependent partners (Capaldo & Giannoccaro, 2015). Moreover, trusting relationships with suppliers can lead to better collaboration, more favorable terms, and increased reliability in the supply chain.

Over time brand recognition and performance credibility are translated into a strong sense of allegiance and memorable interactions that connect customers and suppliers with the brand by tapping into nostalgia, personal values, positive images, or shared purposes. Trust may also become a source of revenue for the organizations, as customers are more likely to make emotional judgments in favor of selecting products and services from trusted sources over competitors. Spillover effects include improved corporate reputation, reduced customer acquisition costs, and mitigated risks. Other benefits include the ability to attract and retain talent and create long-term value proposition for the business.

References

Alemany, C. (2024). Maintaining customer loyalty in the face of inflation. *Harvard Business Review.* Retrieved on October 1, 2025 from https://hbr.org/2024/02/maintaining-customer-loyalty-in-the-face-of-inflation.

Alshareef, S. (2024). https://valar.quantic.edu/blog/2024/11/13/uber-collaborative-leadership-to-employee-empowerment/, November 13.

Avolio, B. J., Gardner, W. L., Walumbwa, F. O., Luthans, F., & May, D. R. (2004). Unlocking the mask: A look at the process by which authentic leaders impact follower attitudes and behaviors. *Leadership Quarterly, 15*(6), 801–823.

Barro, R. J. (1973). The control of politicians: An economic model. *Public Choice, 14*, 19–42 https://doi.org/10.1007/BF01718440.

Belasen, A. T. & Belasen, A. R. (2025). Signaling trust during disruptions: Perceived gender differences in trustworthy leadership traits. *Gender in Management: An International Journal.* https://doi.org/10.1108/GM-04-2024-0187.

Belasen, A. T. & Bertola, L. (2024). Co-creation, strategic visioning, and iterative loops. Chapter 4 in Alan T Belasen & Nicole Pfeffermann (Eds.), *Brilliant Leadership – Unlocking the Power of Innovation-Communication* (pp. 63–77). New York, NY: Routledge.

Capaldo, A. & Giannoccaro, I. (2015). How does trust affect performance in the supply chain? The moderating role of interdependence. *Journal of Supply Chain Management, 166*, 36–49.

Duarte, A. P., Ribeiro, N., Semedo, A. S., & Gomes, D. R. (2021). Authentic leadership and improved individual performance: Affective commitment and individual creativity's sequential mediation. *Frontiers in Psychology, 12*, https://doi.org/10.3389/fpsyg.2021.675749.

Edelman Trust Barometer. (2021). https://www.edelman.com/sites/g/files/aatuss191/files/2021-03/2021%20Edelman%20Trust%20Barometer.pdf.

García-Salirrosas, E. E., Escobar-Farfán, M., Esponda-Perez, J. A., Millones-Liza, D. Y., Villar-Guevara, M., Haro-Zea, K. L., & Gallardo-Canales, R. (2024). The impact of perceived value on brand image and loyalty: A study of healthy food brands in emerging markets. *Frontiers in Nutrition*, *11*, 1482009. https://doi.org/10.3389/fnut.2024.1482009.

Hunt, J. (2023). Trust – The ultimate differentiator. *LinkedIn*, September 5. https://www.linkedin.com/pulse/trust-ultimate-differentiator-goalspan/.

Jun, K., Hu, Z., & Lee, J. (2023). Examining the influence of authentic leadership on follower hope and organizational citizenship behavior: The mediating role of follower identification. *Behavioral sciences (Basel, Switzerland)*, *13*(7), 572. https://doi.org/10.3390/bs13070572.

Kennedy, M. (2024). *LinkedIn*. https://www.linkedin.com/posts/mikekennedy_companies-like-netflix-uber-apple-amazon-activity-7192565560679784448-iXXY/, May 4.

Lorenz, E. N. (1963). Deterministic nonperiodic flow. *Journal of the Atmospheric Sciences*, *20*(2), 130–141.

Price, M. E. & Van Vugt, M. (2014). The evolution of leader-follower reciprocity: the theory of service-for-prestige. *Frontiers in Human Neuroscience*, *8*, 363. https://doi.org/10.3389/fnhum.2014.00363.

Popomaronis, T. (2021). Jeff Bezos on his 4-step method for building trust and reputation: 'It's really that simple'—and research backs it up, CNBC, July 2. https://www.cnbc.com/2021/07/02/jeff-bezos-says-this-is-how-you-earn-trust-and-build-reputation-it-really-is-that-simple.html.

Reina, D. & Reina, M. (2024). Why leadership trust is critical, especially in times of change. *Center for Creative Leadership*, June 15. https://www.ccl.org/articles/leading-effectively-articles/why-leadership-trust-is-critical-in-times-of-change-and-disruption/.

Sanders, R., Bertola, L., & Belasen, A. T. (2024). Driving digital transformation, aligning brand and reputation. Chapter 8 in Alan T Belasen & Nicole Pfeffermann (Eds.), Brilliant *Leadership – Unlocking the Power of Innovation-Communication* (pp. 139–152). New York, NY: Routledge.

Schaub, K. (2023). The butterfly effect: Non-linearity, marketing mysteries, and the human-machine partnership, June. https://www.kathleenschaub.com/blog/butterfly-effect-non-linearity-marketing-human-machine.

Sinek, S. (2011). *Start with Why: How Great Leaders Inspire Everyone to Take Action*. New York: Portfolio/Penguin.

Van Zoonen, W., Sivunen, A. E., & Blomqvist, K. (2024). Out of sight – Out of trust? An analysis of the mediating role of communication frequency and quality in the relationship between workplace isolation and trust. *European Management Journal, 42*(4), 515–526.

Chapter 3

The Roles of Middle and Senior Managers in Building Trust

Introduction

The true test of effective leadership does not occur when everything is running smoothly but rather during disruptive market conditions when divergent thinking, smart choices, and agility enable executives to pivot and adjust strategies swiftly to stay relevant, ultimately giving them a competitive edge over competitors. In stable times, organizational members follow common routines and pre-determined standards that guide their behaviors, actions, and outcomes. The primary function of managers in these organizations is to monitor key performance indicators (KPIs) to track and analyze data and guard against suboptimization. They rely on rules and procedural specifications and apply quality control measures that are aimed at achieving higher levels of internal consistency.

Striving for a higher level of efficiency helps boost organizational reputation as a stable, high reliability organization

 DOI: 10.4324/9781003608028-3

(HRO), although it might impede adaptation. Recall that maintaining a higher level of stability may trigger inertia – an organizational mindset that resists change or limits the ability of the organization to adapt to customer needs or respond quickly to disruptions.

However, major crises or periods of unexpected change disrupt organizational routines and the way individuals and groups perform their tasks, potentially triggering tension over objectives or distrust. This may challenge leaders to reinvent current practices and invest time and efforts in instilling trust and confidence in their abilities to handle disruptions and comfort employees. This is important since building and preserving trust in organizations is also an effective form of organizing, especially during disruptions (Oreg et al., 2018).

Within this context, we explore the critical role of middle managers in managing the tension between these competing commitments and their special contribution to innovation implementation. The primary focus of this chapter is on a framework that establishes the linkage between characteristics of trustworthy leadership and the ability to lead during disruptive times. As we point out – cultivating attributes of *transparency*, *accountability*, *credibility*, and *honesty* enables organizational leaders to hone the skills needed to be viewed by employees and stakeholders as being trustworthy and prepared for the unexpected.

Disruptive Change

During disruptions, the trust that employees have in their leaders influences the interpretation of uncertainty and helps to reduce employees' perceived threat as they believe in the ability of trustworthy leaders to create safe environments. Leaders whose words and deeds are incongruent will find it challenging to rebuild trust during episodes of disruption (Belasen &

Belasen, 2019). When employees lose trust in their leaders, they experience decreased productivity, low morale and disengagement, holding back information and reluctance to share new ideas, rise in stress levels, and general feelings of insecurity.

An SHRM (2024) survey reveals that a significant number of employees are experiencing negative effects from work-related stress, with 44% feeling burn out at work, 45% feeling "emotionally drained," and 51% feeling "used up" at the end of the workday. This continued the trend from the SHRM (2023) survey in which 57% of employees surveyed reported feelings of burnout symptoms like emotional exhaustion affecting their productivity and engagement levels.

The SHRM surveys were consistent with the results of the earlier American Psychological Association (APA, 2023) Work in America Survey which confirmed that psychological safety is highly valued by 57% of the sampled employees with 66% of all respondents indicating that it is very important for them to feel respected at work. Higher stress levels can impair memory and cognitive abilities, leading to errors, added negative emotions, and lower motivation.

The American Institute of Stress reports that job stress costs US employers more than $300 billion annually due to absenteeism, turnover, decreased productivity, and related healthcare and insurance costs. Globally, an estimated 12 billion working days are lost every year due to work-related depression and anxiety at a cost of US$ 1 trillion per year in lost productivity (WHO, 2024).

DISRUPTIVE CHANGE IS HITTING LEADERS and MANAGERS HARDEST

Seven in ten US workers reported disruptive change within their organization in the last year, according to a nationally representative Gallup survey of 18,665 employees. Twenty percent of respondents cited a large or very large extent of change. These

> changes range from restructuring efforts to shifting return-to-office expectations to new leadership and more.
>
> While difficulties often affect frontline workers, in the current business landscape, it's leaders and managers who are experiencing the most change. Leaders and managers are 56% more likely to experience extensive disruptive change in their organization than [employees]…Over half of managers state their organization has restructured teams, while nearly half say they've had to make budget cuts.
>
> A 2023 Gallup [survey] found that managers today are more likely than non-managers to be disengaged at work, burnt out, looking for a new job or feeling like their organization doesn't care about their wellbeing. These changes strain interpersonal relationships. Employees reporting extensive disruptive change are 67% more likely to cite an issue with a leader or manager.
>
> Many of the disruptions that employees cite result from leadership decisions intended to benefit the organization long term. However, change can be unsettling and tumultuous...Employees who report experiencing disruptive change are less engaged and less connected to their organization's culture. They are also more likely to be burnt out and to leave their employer. Among those employees who cited significant disruption [in 2023], those who strongly agreed that they trusted the leadership of their organization were 4.5 times as likely to be engaged and 62% less likely to feel burned out at work.
>
> Among those same disrupted employees, those who strongly agreed their leaders communicate effectively with the rest of their organization…were 4.3 times as likely to be engaged and 65% less likely to feel frequently burned out at work (Barrett & Kemp, 2024).

Employees may be hesitant to take risks or openly communicate concerns as distrust in leaders starts to creep up with diminished confidence that leaders are too ambiguous, do not have the ability to deliver goods, nor do they have a genuine interest in the growth of employees. As an SHRM (2023) researcher observed: “If you consider how many workers are feeling burned out and the direct and indirect effects burnout has on an organization, it should really raise a red flag to organizational leaders.”

To reengage and become fully committed, employees expect their leaders to be trustworthy, listen to their concerns, be respectful, transparent, and empathetic. These simple expectations are not too difficult to accomplish through relational activities and reciprocal trust, especially since a lack of trust can have a significant effect on a company, its leaders, and its employees. What signifies the problem, however, is a new forecast by DDI (2025) showing that from 2022 to 2024, trust in immediate managers has been dwindling from 46% to 29% of employees fully trusting their direct managers to do what is right.

WHAT HAPPENS WHEN EMPLOYEES NO LONGER TRUST THEIR LEADERSHIP?

Employees Stop Listening

When employees' trust in their leaders erodes, they stop listening to their advice. People do not do what you want them to do just because you tell them to do it. If people cannot trust your word, quite simply, they are unlikely to listen to it. When a leader demonstrates inconsistency between what they say and what they do, their employees can see that. The overarching message is that your word is not trustworthy – or that not doing what you say you will is somehow acceptable.

Employees Disengage

An employee engagement initiative won't work if there is a fundamental lack of trust that underlies it. When employees do not trust their leaders, they check out emotionally and mentally. When employees check out, they are more likely to quit when a new opportunity arises. This kind of disengagement often means that employees will do the bare minimum to get by, at best. And at worst, disengaged employees can become toxic and hostile to the company.

Employees Stop Innovating

When employees do not trust their leaders, they become unwilling to innovate, speak up, or take calculated risks. Trust is a fundamental part of psychological safety, the shared belief that teamwork spaces are safe for interpersonal risk-taking. When employees don't trust that their leaders will have their backs – whether they challenge something in the workplace or simply ask for help – they begin to feel unsafe. If that's the case, productivity plummets and inefficiency thrive.

Miscommunication Happens

If there is a lack of trust, employees are likely to build walls to protect themselves. Even if they work well with their own team, they are unlikely to try to collaborate outside of their immediate circle. This has a negative impact on interteam communication, which can increase the likelihood of mistakes. As the quality of work drops or things are done incorrectly, frustration grows and can even lead to conflict (Fast Company, 2024).

Trustworthy leaders influence followers through the demonstration of benevolence, high personal integrity, and behavioral tendencies, which endure even when the leaders are absent. Leaders need to be sensitive and attuned to moments of difference and feel responsible for working with those differences. Trusting relationships are sustained when leaders focus on common purposes, are inspirational, and project trustworthiness and empathy that ensure that people stay calm and engaged.

Facilitating Change

Middle managers make substantial qualitative and quantitative contributions to their organizations and have the know-how to move work forward with tact and velocity. They understand the complexity of work environments and are well suited to dealing with diverse stakeholders. They engage in dual lines of reporting with top-down implementation roles and bottom-up facilitation roles. Middle managers' operating experience coupled with proximity to senior executives make their unique contributions critical for achieving success. Positioned between corporate executives and frontline leaders, they can provide much richer perspectives on technical tasks involving operations and compliance, monitor employee behaviors and key interactions, and clarify strategic objectives associated with financial reports, analysis, and implementation.

Functioning as intermediaries across hierarchical levels, middle managers must strike a delicate balance between creativity and efficiency, and between inspirational and project management roles. Middle managers accomplish this through synthesizing information as well as championing and executing plans (Belasen & Rufer, 2013). Synthesizing information consists of gathering intelligence on the feasibility of new programs, sharing intelligence about competitors and suppliers with top executives as well as prioritizing new trends in the business environment.

When the strategic vision is articulated clearly, middle managers through their know-how, experience, and networking can play a more active role aligning planning with implementation. They help facilitate the need for change in communications with executives and help implement innovation in interactions with lower levels. Implementing innovation requires an effective balance of strategic awareness with operating experience and an optimal mix of leadership and management roles, allowing them to see beyond immediate issues and make decisions based on a wide perspective.

Balancing competing demands is important as diverse stakeholders often place different claims against the goals and strategies of the organization. A broader perspective gives leaders and teams permission to engage in opposing strategies – to exploit existing products and services while simultaneously exploring new offerings and business models. Middle managers more so than senior managers or frontline leaders have the competence to handle the complexity of information and the number of potential interactions.

Middle managers are not just the pivot point on which an organization pivots but serve as the lynch pin that at times holds the organization together when it is pulled in opposite directions between marketing and operations, manufacturing and sales, and top-down and bottom-up communications. Senior executives who recognize the complexity of middle management roles, also make efforts to enlist and leverage the strengths of middle managers.

These executives prioritize transparency, actively listen to middle managers' concerns, demonstrate accountability in decision-making, acknowledge the limits of their competence, avoid overconfidence by empowering middle managers to contribute, and consistently follow through on commitments, promoting a culture of trust. By understanding the boundaries of their own knowledge and by seeking out additional expertise from middle managers, senior executives strengthen the trusting relationships within the administrative structure (Atir & Dunning, 2024).

Diminished Value

Recently, however, the value of middle managers has come under attack. Despite their valuable contributions middle managers have been viewed as "forgotten practitioners" and an occupation whose autonomy is largely constrained. The constant pressure on middle managers to focus on daily routines away from strategic circles often placed them in sink-or-swim situations, forcing them to figure out expectations, leading to potential failure if they couldn't act quickly or perform effectively. Moreover, as technological advances and social media allow executives to know more about customers' preferences, the roles of middle manager have been squeezed from all directions.

In fact, some detractors have gone as far as calling for delayering the supervision structure by removing middle management from organizations. Delayering creates spillover effects with a larger span of control for executives and with added responsibilities for the remaining managers who are expected to deal with tactical, operational issues.

Given the hardship inevitably faced by middle managers, it should come as no surprise that they are often blamed for organizational failures. This is because the organizational "work" they are charged with carrying out is interconnected and too difficult to evaluate individually. Frustrated middle managers often react by sliding out to isolated, out-of-reach positions. Unable to handle cross-over pressures, they tend to stay away or lay low, in effect choosing an avoidance strategy and unintentionally fueling the image of disengaged or uncommitted managers (Belasen & Belasen, 2017).

The way executives relate to middle managers is subtly influenced by their own expectations or perceived trustworthiness embodied in the relationship. If they expect mediocre performance – it will lead to lowering the bar in expectation of poor performance. This also creates a vicious cycle in which the initial perception of uncommitted middle managers is reinforced. They are perceived as mediocre or weak performers who tend to live down to the low expectations that senior executives have set out for them, in effect perpetuating the (wrong) view of incompetence.

This self-reinforcing process, prime for conditions of failure, is also known as the *Pygmalion Effect.* Pygmalion refers to a person who consciously or unconsciously is aware of an expectation and acts in a way that is consistent with that expectation. In the context of management, the Pygmalion Effect refers to how a senior executive's low expectations can result in decreased performance, essentially creating a self-fulfilling prophecy where middle managers tend to live up (or down) to the executive's beliefs about their abilities (Belasen & Belasen, 2017).

Rebuilding Trust

Disruptions can magnify leadership vulnerabilities, particularly how leaders access, understand, and react to new sources of information. Equally important is regaining employees' confidence by encouraging them to trust the leaders' ability to deal with workplace disruptions. Trustworthy executives who are aware of their vulnerabilities can improve their relationships with middle managers using trust–repair strategies. These may include changing their mindsets about how they value the contributions of middle managers, adjusting ground rules and norms of behavior, modeling desired behaviors, communicating clear expectations, and updating metrics for evaluating middle managers' performance. Informal means may be anchored in messaging that incorporates collective values, organizational identity, brand image, culture and history.

SEVEN LEADERSHIP BEHAVIORS TO BUILD TRUST

Employees perform their best when they trust their leaders. We found that leaders who trust their senior leaders are nearly three times more likely to develop novel ideas or solutions than those in low trust organizations. They are also less concerned with failing and try new ideas as an opportunity to learn. Opportunities to strengthen trust happen in everyday interactions. We found seven behaviors that improve trust perceptions when leaders do them more frequently. In order of impact, these behaviors are as follows:

1. Listen and respond with empathy.
2. Provide opportunities for team members' growth and development.
3. Share thoughts and rationale for decisions.
4. Genuinely acknowledge your own failures.
5. Inquire and care about employee wellbeing.
6. Encourage others to challenge old ways of doing things.
7. Recognize the success of team members.

In our analysis, 85% of employees who indicated that their leaders consistently did these things reported that they trusted their managers to do what is right.

In addition to these seven leader behaviors, we found a relationship between trust and a leader's willingness to be vulnerable. When leaders regularly display vulnerability, their employees are 5.3 times more likely to trust them. Furthermore, when leaders genuinely acknowledge their failures or shortcomings, they were 7.5 times more likely to maintain trust over those that did not. Leaders often fear that displaying vulnerability may be interpreted as weakness. But the data is clear that leaders who are self-aware about their imperfections build stronger relationships with their teams (DDI, 2023).

When top-down communication is clear, empathetic, transparent, and frequent, internal dialogues are more positive and middle managers are likely to show more confidence in their own ability to perform their duties and, at the same time, trust the ability of executives to cocreate – to jointly develop ideas, solutions, and outcomes. Balancing control with autonomy is key. When senior leaders actively engage middle managers, provide them with clear direction during disruptions, and show genuine concern for their well-being, trust is more likely to be established, fostering a shared sense of ownership and responsibility in the process.

Dimensions of Trust

Executives who work with middle managers on a well-synchronized communication delivery plan that includes responses to warning signals of a threatening situation also build good working relationships with middle managers. To prolong these relationships, middle managers, the direct reports of senior executives, also seek assurances that those above them, the senior executives who manage them and assess their performance, are competent and trustworthy.

This is where reciprocal trust in which executives and middle managers rely on each other to act honestly, reliably, and with good intentions, becomes a two-way process where both sides need to actively demonstrate trustworthiness. To sustain these relationships over the long haul, they must be **credible**, **transparent**, and carried out by leaders who project high levels of personal integrity and **honesty** and who inspire joint **accountability** (Belasen & Belasen, 2025).

When the perceptions of trustworthiness across senior executives and middle managers align, they also promote understanding and cooperation with both levels of management sharing common vision, priorities, and communication style, ensuring a seamless execution of strategies and an effective coordination of activities across functional units (Figure 3.1). Misaligned perceptions (i.e., when executives view middle managers as less trustworthy) may trigger unclear messages from executives and misunderstandings among middle managers. In turn, this may lead to excessive oversight from executives, further stifling initiatives and creativity in middle managers.

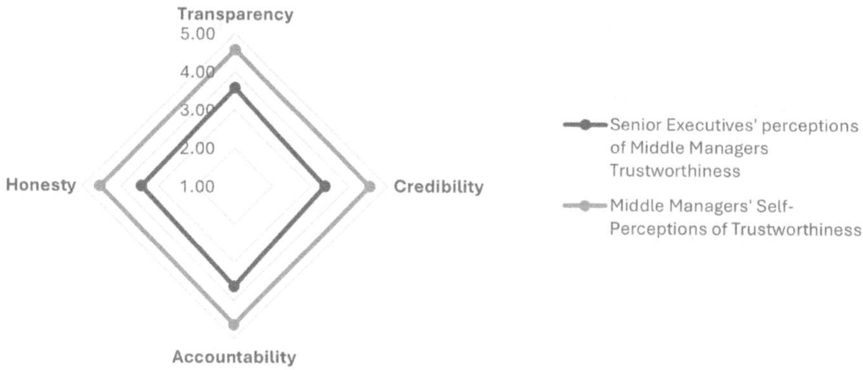

Figure 3.1 Perceptions of Trustworthiness

Credibility reinforces important goals and interests and the need to be open to feedback and when needed to delegate responsibilities to employees. A leader's credibility depends on the perceptions of their honesty and personal integrity, demonstrated competence, and consistency in values and actions, showing that their behaviors align with their words and that they can be trusted to make sound judgment and delivering results.

Leaders are the "face" of the organization to stakeholders, both internally and externally. Externally, they shape the brand image by promoting consistent quality, trustworthiness, and ability to deliver reliable products and services resulting in greater customer loyalty and a positive brand reputation. Internally, they influence norms of behavior and performance expectations by setting the tone, and by actively establishing a positive workplace climate. Thoughts such as, "I could do it better" will creep into employees' cognition if they perceive their leaders as credible and trustworthy.

Trust promotes leadership reputation. When employees perceive their leader's actions and behaviors as trustworthy, it significantly contributes to a more positive view of the organization's reputation. Employees who view their leader as trustworthy and view the organization more positively as a whole are more engaged, leading to increased productivity and better overall performance. People at high-trust companies report 74% less stress, 106% more energy at work, 50% higher productivity, 13% fewer sick days, 76% more engagement, 29% more satisfaction with their lives, and 40% less burnout than people at low-trust companies (Zak, 2017).

Transparency allows leaders to keep everyone informed and involved. It helps build trust with employees, fosters open communication, encourages teamwork, and creates a positive work environment where people feel safe to share ideas and give feedback. Transparent leaders promote diversity in decision-making processes and improve employee engagement and productivity. Transparency also demonstrates integrity by openly sharing both success stories and willingness to learn from failure.

Transparency further reflects the courage of leaders to be vulnerable due to the exposed nature of how leaders are perceived by others. To increase trust, leaders must be more open and transparent with their communications, especially since employees perceive trust and distrust through the lenses of quality communication and personal job security (Saunders et al., 2014).

Transparent leaders benefit from having strong self-awareness skills, being authentic by showing their true self, and having the moral courage to reveal their vulnerability. These leaders trust their intuition. They gain support by demonstrating intuitive intelligence and by knowing how to "read" events and people quickly, sense and understand the emotions and needs of others, and figure out the best responses to pressing issues without needing to rely on much explicit data. They draw on life experiences and gut feelings to make informed decisions, particularly in complex or rapidly changing environments.

Honesty is a trait that fosters trust between leaders and followers, builds credibility in the relationship, and encourages open and positive communication. Honesty is also considered an essential part of a leader's emotional intelligence skills as it allows followers to believe in their leader's words and actions. Leaders with strong self-regulation and empathy skills know when to be open and honest and when to keep their feelings to themselves. Self-regulation involves the ability to manage emotions, behaviors, and thoughts in challenging situations, enabling leaders to respond appropriately, keep their focus and stay calm even when faced with major disruptions.

These leaders are perceived as trustworthy, because they demonstrate high personal integrity, are empathetic with those who are affected by their decisions, are adept at picking up subtle cues, and adapt their responses while still considering rational analysis. Honesty allows leaders to promote openness and ownership of decisions and outcomes, while holding members to high standards of truthfulness.

Accountability reflects the importance of complying with regulations, disseminating relevant messages, and communicating timely information or actionable items to stakeholders.

Accountable leaders are expected to set SMART objectives, take responsibility for both successes and failures, address failures constructively and use learning to grow, actively communicate with individuals and teams, and get others involved in problem solving. SMART objectives involve setting up Specific, Measurable, Achievable, Relevant, and Time-bound tasks and responsibilities that enhance ownership and accountability.

Accountability strengthens the bond of trust and cooperation between leaders and followers. Effective leaders are expected to model trust not through a "blind trust," but rather a "smart trust" with clear expectations and a strong sense of accountability that are built in joint activities (Covey, 2008).

Trust is shown when specific expectations guarantee that those who are trusted behave accordingly. Thus, accountability reflects a personal commitment that helps a leader to measure up to expectations and manage the risks of rewards and losses when placing trust in an actor (Herne et al., 2022).

Trustworthy leaders project **credibility** and **honesty** by prioritizing organizational needs above their own, and by creating a safe and inclusive environment where organizational members feel valued and respected. They foster **transparent** communications and demonstrate personal **accountability** by reflecting on inputs from others and by following through to see things to the end. Cultivating the traits of transparency, honesty, credibility, and accountability enables leaders to have the awareness to build trust and be prepared for disruptions. The following sections elaborate on these characteristics.

What Is My Trustworthiness Score?

The trustworthy leadership assessment described in the following text reflects the dimensions that comprise the framework discussed throughout the book – *Transparency*, *Accountability*, *Credibility*, and *Honesty*. The survey questions address the extent to which managers focus on using inclusive leadership, are sensitive to stakeholders, whether they encourage feedback and joint decision making, and how well they hold themselves to high ethical standards.

Self-assessment and self-improvement relate to the process of self-regulation. Self-regulation involves the exertion of self-control through (a) the setting of internal standards, which can be existing standards or newly formulated ones, (b) the evaluation of discrepancies between these standards and actual or potential outcomes, and (c) the identification of intended actions for resolving these discrepancies (Gardner et al., 2005: 354). A leader's inability to self-regulate, acknowledge gaps, or initiate a shift from the current mindset or behavior to the acceptable level (one that is appreciated or recognized publicly) might potentially lead to failure.

The survey items in Table 3.1 are designed to capture the dimensions of trustworthiness by addressing the extent to which managers focus on using collaborative leadership style, are sensitive to stakeholders, whether they encourage feedback and joint decision-making, and how well they hold themselves to high ethical standards (Belasen & Belasen, 2025).

This 40-item assessment reflects the values associated with transparency, credibility, accountability, and honesty and consists of Likert-style response options with answers on a scale of 1 (I do not demonstrate this behavior) to 5 (I demonstrate this behavior to a great degree). Respondents are asked to answer the questions twice, first as a manifestation of their "actual" behavior; and second, as a reflection of their "desired" behavior. The example in Figure 3.2 transposes the two sets of responses to provide a single view of the gaps across the four dimensions of trustworthy leadership.

Assessment – Trustworthy Leadership

Rate each item on a scale from 1 to 5 where:

1 – I do not demonstrate this behavior
2 – I demonstrate this behavior to a small degree
3 – I demonstrate this behavior to a moderate degree
4 – I demonstrate this behavior frequently
5 – I demonstrate this behavior to a great degree

Next, rate yourself again, this time by considering your improvement and growth goals. Understandably, the ratings in Figure 3.2, which denote current behaviors, are lower than the ratings which represent desired or future behaviors. The gap between the two sets signifies opportunities for improvement.

Table 3.1 Trustworthy Leadership Questionnaire

	Actual	*Desired*
Transparency		
I feel my goals are accepted by others		
I strive to achieve successful outcomes through participation		
I pay close attention to how well I work with others		
I use a plan that is shared publicly and that guides the collective performance		
I make sure that we understand each other's concerns		
I seek to understand the needs of my followers		
I revise my vision and goals based on inputs from diverse stakeholders		
AVERAGE		
Credibility		
I am candid and openly express my thoughts and concerns		
I articulate shared goals and interests consistently		
I tell the truth with high conviction		
When I withhold information, I let people know the reason		
I consistently share personal commitments in the open		
I admit to personal mistakes and do not blame others for my failure		
I listen to others attentively		
I welcome constructive criticisms		

(*Continued*)

Table 3.1 (Continued) Trustworthy Leadership Questionnaire

At times of change I remain open to new ideas		
I value feedback from others even if it negates my thinking		
I ask stakeholders for ideas to improve organizational performance		
AVERAGE		
Accountability		
I clarify my actions to various stakeholders		
I encourage employees to explain our values to stakeholders		
I emphasize the importance of complying with regulations fairly and objectively		
I strive to ensure that we openly and accountably share practices and outcomes		
I emphasize the obligation of carrying out government policies properly		
I ensure that we follow rules and procedures consistently and equitably		
I adhere to ethical codes of conduct		
I communicate and reinforce integrity guidelines		
I clarify the personal and collective consequences of misconduct		
I take responsibility for the outcomes of my decisions or behaviors		
I support diversity, equity, and inclusion goals		
AVERAGE		
Honesty		
I am approachable when others need me		

(*Continued*)

Table 3.1 (Continued) Trustworthy Leadership Questionnaire

I support giving back to the community		
I encourage everyone to participate in decision making		
I act with respect and demonstrate integrity in the workplace		
I seek to meet others' expectations of me		
I hold myself and others to high ethical standards		
I put others' best interests above my own		
I have a thorough understanding of organizational values		
I would not compromise ethical principles to gain personal benefits		
I make sincere efforts to know about others' career goals		
I value honesty more than profit		
AVERAGE		

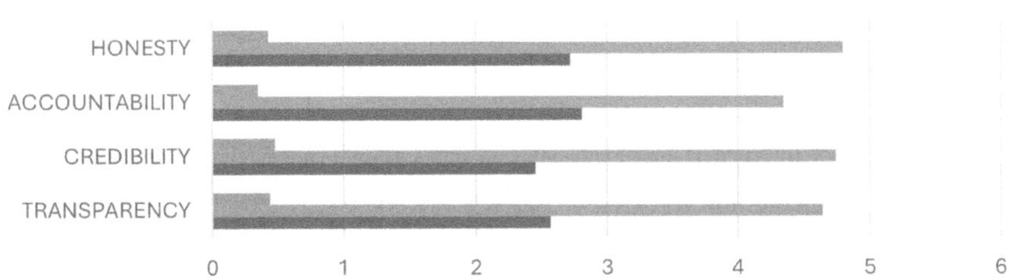

	TRANSPARENCY	CREDIBILITY	ACCOUNTABILITY	HONESTY
■ Gap	45%	48%	35%	43%
■ Desired	4.65	4.75	4.35	4.8
■ Current	2.57	2.45	2.81	2.72

Figure 3.2 Trustworthy Leadership: Actual Versus Desired Traits

To bridge the gap between actual and desired behaviors, self-assessments can be used periodically to see how well respondents progressed over time (Belasen & Eisenberg, 2023). Another option is to obtain feedback from direct reports, peers, or supervisors. Senior executives and board members can use the survey to assess middle managers' trustworthiness across the four dimensions and, if needed, serve as mentors to help middle managers improve their behaviors across the dimensions.

The differences between self-assessment and assessment from senior executives could be very revealing and should lead to a more valid and reliable understanding of how well middle managers are perceived and the steps they need to take to meet expectations. Subsequently, ideas and actions for improvement could be prioritized to reflect input from senior executives and eventually lead to improved relationships across hierarchical levels and functional lines (Belasen & Rufer, 2013).

The dimensions of trustworthy leadership must be present simultaneously to increase the propensity to act with trust. A gap in **transparency** occurs when a leader is micro-oriented, focusing attention on monitoring the flow of communication or withholding information until necessary, prioritizing control and secrecy in communication, often used during disruption. While these are important matters and they cannot be ignored, the temptation among some middle managers is to act with a sense of urgency rather than strategy. Unfortunately, this is also when strengths become weaknesses – when they are overused or misapplied.

A gap in transparency can be overcome by reinforcing a culture of open and clear communication, actively sharing information, and interacting and fostering a culture of trust where people feel safe probing questions or providing feedback.

A gap in **accountability** is usually marked by a tendency to shoot from the hip, resulting in making solo decisions without the benefit of consulting with others. Middle managers who wish to improve in this area need to resist the temptation to make decisions quickly. Unless the matter is extremely urgent and a decision absolutely must be made on the spot, leaders should pause and explore the likely risks and costs of making the wrong decision. Other opportunities to improve include leading by example and holding yourself accountable first; setting clear expectations, developing active listening, giving and receiving feedback; and establishing two-way communication processes.

A gap in **honesty** may prove to be the most difficult to remedy, since it relies on the individual's self-regulation and the ability to empathize with others. Bosses have a tremendous impact on those who work in an organization. Recent surveys of employees have found extremely high levels of dissatisfaction with workplaces that are saturated with dishonesty.

Simply by being transparent in their communications across hierarchical levels, consistently following through on their commitments, admitting mistakes when they occur, middle managers can improve their perceived honesty. Leading by example with ethical behavior and upholding high standards of integrity within the workplace, acknowledging mistakes, praising others in public and giving credit where credit is due, and following up in a timely manner are simple but important ways to improve the perception of personal integrity.

Finally, a gap in **credibility** leads to a tarnished reputation and a negative view of managers as political and manipulative. These leaders tend to withhold information, resort to secrecy and closed-door decisions. Trustworthy managers who lead by example are not only true to themselves but also help others to become more credible by consistently demonstrating honesty, competence, and transparency in their actions.

When middle managers actively listen to their teams, follow through on actions by keeping promises, learning from failures, taking responsibility, and aligning their words with their deeds – they also build credibility with executives and employees and earn their trust.

Putting It In Action – A Middle Manager's Account

Results of my current profile for trustworthy leadership (Figure 3.3) reflect honesty as my highest strength and credibility as my weakest area. Transparency and accountability fall in the middle with almost equal scoring. Honesty as my highest strength did not come as a surprise as I've always had a strong proclivity for being honest and telling the truth. At times I've been told I'm too honest, but ultimately, I believe one cannot be faulted for being truthful in comparison to lying and hiding facts. I mindfully consider the consequences of not being honest as I would never want to jeopardize my employment or my character. I work in compliance which naturally calls for honesty and transparency to help save the organization from possible risks.

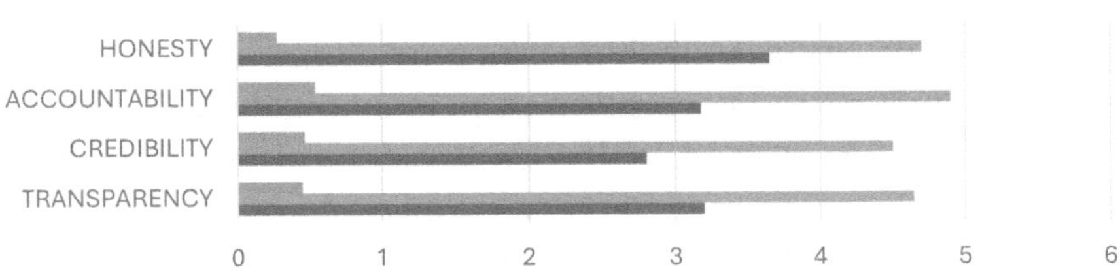

	TRANSPARENCY	CREDIBILITY	ACCOUNTABILITY	HONESTY
■ Gap	45%	47%	54%	28%
■ Desired	4.65	4.5	4.9	4.7
■ Current	3.2	2.8	3.18	3.65

Figure 3.3 Middle Manager's Current and Desired Ratings

I questioned my results within the area of credibility as I see myself as someone who is dependable and sticks to their word. I consider myself to have moral and ethical values and strive to be fair and empathetic. I do my best to follow through on promises and guarantees and strive to be a resource for the business areas I am accountable for.

After studying the results of my assessment, I realized there is in fact room for improvement as I tend to keep my thoughts and decision-making processes – although ethical and moral – to myself. Because of this, I imagine it can be difficult for others to understand where I am coming from and how I reach certain decisions. My relatively lack of sharing feedback probably creates more confusion and questions than intended which can affect the trust others have in me.

I have no problem working in groups and collaborating with others, but the spotlight is not what I strive for. I am a team player who is willing to take on new challenges and support changes for the greater good, however, innovative thinking is not my strongest suit and I am not usually the one to offer new ideas. I am responsible for overseeing my business areas in terms of regulatory compliance and guidance, but I am not expected to dictate how the business area completes their work to become compliant. This dynamic can cause some friction since it can come off as making demands or creating more work without providing additional help. I must work to find innovative, creative ways to challenge and inspire them to meet goals without creating confusion and frustration.

Openly asking for feedback and actively working to improve my performance will strengthen my credibility, build trust, and improve my relationships over time. Being more consistent in how I provide information as well as my thought processes will help eliminate confusion and strengthen their understanding of my role. I also plan to develop myself as a transformational leader by encouraging frontline leaders to transcend their own interests for the good of the organization. A small change I plan on making is turning on my camera more often when working from home to help strengthen our communication and encourage engagement as many social cues are lost during virtual meetings. Overall, my hope is to improve my standing as a trustworthy leader for my areas of responsibility by being more outwardly honest, reliable, and transparent in the way I communicate.

Middle Managers' Reflections

The following sections, with minor edits, are excerpts from exchanges among middle managers participating in a leadership development program with a focus on leading with trust.

Middle Manager A – As expected, current levels did not meet target levels in any category. Overall, it appears the category of transparency is the closest to being aligned with the desired threshold, while accountability has the greatest disparity. I believe the first step in improving trusted leadership traits is self-awareness. One must be willing to continually analyze one's own actions and the reactions of others to gauge how behavior is being perceived. Once lessons are learned, integrity and other associated traits can be internalized through self-regulation. By remembering what one has learned through observation, an individual should be able to better control their behavior and choose actions that inspire trust in others.

A challenge in the improvement plan is being honest with oneself. It is a tempting reflex to blame others for the negative perceptions that one experiences. I believe this is especially true regarding traits such as honesty and integrity, as perceived shortcomings have a deeply personal quality. It is important to remember, also, that having honest intentions is not enough, they must also be effectively communicated and demonstrated, or else perceptions cannot be improved.

In my professional life, finding mentorship can be challenging. I work for a large and widely dispersed organization where much of the daily work is completed by self-sufficient and somewhat isolated teams or individuals. While I enjoy this autonomy, there are few opportunities to cultivate friendships or mentorships. However, I do maintain close contact with previous peers. I believe these friends can be a valuable resource for self-improvement consultations and discussions. We have worked together in the past, yet they are all detached from my present professional environment so they can provide fair and honest feedback.

Peer 1 – It was interesting to read your results from the trustworthy leadership survey and see your areas for improvement. I think you made a great point that it is human nature to blame others when something doesn't go well. Having self-awareness and the ability to reflect on the situation and your fault in it is very valuable. That is something I want to work on as well. Taking time to reflect on how you can help things go better in the future is a very important step in self-improvement.

I agree with you that finding mentorship in the workplace can be challenging. At my previous employer this was not something that was prioritized. However, at my current job there is a mentorship program which I have found to be immensely helpful. I have an assigned mentor that was set up by HR. It is a relatively new program that has seen positive results. Maybe this is something you could bring up and discuss with your HR department.

Peer 2 – I like how you mentioned your current company does not offer a mentorship program, but you have reached out to prior colleagues instead. This can be beneficial as they have an outside perspective and may be able to assist you in your development without being involved in your day-to-day work. I do feel that as times are changing, having mentorship or leadership programs available is beneficial to the growth of an organization. These programs can help to reduce turnover and help to ensure organizations retain stronger leaders who understand the working of the organization, as opposed to hiring leaders from outside who do not have a full understanding of the business.

Working for an organization myself for 10 years that had the view of "you do what you were hired to do" without growth strategies and then going to an organization that encourages growth by having mentorship and leadership training, was eye opening for me personally. It was difficult to understand at first because it was new, but now it makes me feel like my leadership aspirations for the future are obtainable, and I do have the support in getting to where I want to be with the help of my senior managers.

Peer 3 – I agree with your comment regarding how honest intentions are not enough. It reminded me of the saying "We judge others by their actions and ourselves by our intentions." What we *intend* is not necessarily how others will perceive our actions. I also agree with your point that our *intentions* must be effectively communicated and demonstrated to assist in ensuring others' perceptions of us align with our intentions.

I can relate to your situation where your position is largely self-sufficient and thus there are few opportunities to find mentors – as I am also in a position that is largely autonomous by nature, but I have been able to forge strong working relationships with colleagues on the same "level" as me. The important part is to find trusted colleagues to provide feedback on performance and leadership behaviors so we can identify our personal strengths and areas of improvement. Once we know our areas of improvement, we can then use our trusted colleagues to assist us in goal setting and building development plans to achieve those goals.

Peer 4 – Using the bar graph to analyze the gap between current and target levels is a thoughtful way to pinpoint areas for improvement. Transparency emerging as the closest aligned category indicates you already have a foundation to build upon, while the disparity in accountability shows an opportunity for growth. The current leadership development highlights the importance of aligning individual and organizational behavior to foster trust, emphasizing consistency and credibility as key elements in leadership development.

You correctly identify self-awareness as the starting point for improving leadership traits. Just as leaders must analyze market dynamics to adapt strategies, they must evaluate their own behaviors to foster trust. Regular self-assessment, paired with genuine feedback from colleagues or mentors, can lead to stronger personal accountability and transparency. This mirrors your point about observing the reactions of others and learning from them.

Middle Manager B – Reflecting on the results of my assessment, I observed that my lowest score was in accountability, while my highest was in honesty. This aligns well with my professional background in financial compliance, a field where honesty is critical. However, accurately assessing my accountability proved challenging, as my current role rarely presents opportunities to demonstrate these behaviors. As a result, I tended to assign lower scores, typically 2 or 3, for questions that did not align with my present experiences.

The survey results highlight my strong desire to improve in areas such as transparency and credibility, where I have set my target scores at 4s and 5s. This ambition stems from understanding the critical role these attributes play in building trust within a team. My current manager's feedback supports my self-assessment, as he rated me higher in transparency (3.57 vs. 3.14) and credibility (3.91 vs. 3.45) than I did, while noting that my accountability score was slightly lower than my self-rating (2.82 vs. 2.91). This feedback underscores the need for me to actively seek opportunities to demonstrate accountability, especially as I prepare for a future senior leadership role.

To improve my overall profile, I plan to engage in targeted professional development. This includes seeking feedback from peers and mentors, participating in leadership training programs, and actively practicing decision-making in simulated environments. Research indicates that leaders who engage in continuous learning and seek feedback are more likely to enhance their leadership effectiveness. Additionally, I aim to develop a structured approach to risk management, which will involve analyzing potential risks and developing contingency plans.

Sustaining my desired leadership profile presents several challenges. One significant challenge is the dynamic nature of organizational environments, which can shift rapidly due to external pressures such as market changes or technological advancements. This volatility can test the resilience of my leadership qualities and the trust I have built with my team. Furthermore, maintaining a balance between authority and approachability is crucial; as I strive to be a trusted leader, I must ensure that my decisions are respected while remaining accessible to my team.

To guide my improvement efforts, I have identified a mentor who exemplifies trusted leadership. This individual has a proven track record of fostering trust within their organization and has successfully navigated challenges like those I face. By engaging with this mentor, I can gain insights into effective leadership strategies and receive constructive feedback on my development journey.

Peer 1 – It is great that you have created clear goals with action plans to achieve them. You also already have a trusted mentor to help you with your professional development journey. With your results from the assessment and your personal analysis, you have a solid foundation to start with.

I recommend you ask your trusted mentor to also take the assessment to confirm your results and possibly identify any gaps that might have resulted from unknown personal biases.

With the results of both, you can work with your mentor to create a career development plan and identify professional opportunities within your organization for you to gain experience in your areas of development and further experience in your strengths.

Peer 2 – The point you have made about dynamic environments is interesting. Change is a stressor to both individuals and organizations. It can be challenging to know where the change is heading at times, creating challenges for transparent communication. In such situations, it may not be that people are purposefully secretive, it is just that no one knows what is going on!

We have a large project involving energy efficiency. Much of this project was catalyzed by local building code changes, presenting a regulatory component to the design creating an environment where different teams were operating under different paradigms. These dynamics have slowly morphed into a situation where information sharing was compromised, with each team reluctant to have their "worldview" regarding this project challenged.

In my opinion, in addition to the need for clear project requirements, this situation demonstrates the need for senior leadership with clear vision and the ability to communicate said vision. Without this, it is difficult to achieve project alignment, and the final deliverable ends up compromised in some way.

Middle Manager B's response – That's a great observation, and I think you're touching on a fundamental challenge in any complex project, especially one influenced by shifting regulations. The combination of uncertainty and varying interpretations of requirements can easily create silos, as you've described. It is not that teams are intentionally withholding information; it's more about protecting their interpretation or framework when there's no clear consensus.

Your point about leadership is spot on. In situations like this, having a leader with a clear vision and the ability to articulate it in a way that unifies the team is critical. They don't necessarily need to have all the answers themselves, but they need to provide a framework that allows teams to align their efforts and navigate the uncertainty together. This could include encouraging regular cross-group communication, creating spaces where disagreements or misalignments can be discussed constructively, and ensuring everyone stays focused on the shared goals of the project rather than their individual group's perspective.

Middle Manager C – Of the four categories my highest score was accountability and my lowest was for transparency. Overall, I was pleased with my current results, but I know there are areas for improvement considering my aspirations for promotion. One area is credibility. I know that I am not the best at asking for feedback. I am always looking for the end goal and completion of a project without taking the extra step of asking for feedback. Additionally, I have struggled with constructive criticisms, taking it too personally. This is something I need to be aware of and work on improving going forward.

Another area of improvement is transparency and specifically making others aware of the vision and progress of the project. It is easy for me to get wrapped up in a project. I need to take a step back and make sure that others are aware of what is happening. Also, I need to do a better job of touching base with the stakeholders during the project to make sure we are on the right track.

Currently I have a mentor at my job. I think I could leverage their thoughts on ideas for improving my scores. Having someone to hold me accountable on this would be a great way to make sure I am prioritizing these improvements.

Peer 1 – In response to your comment on taking constructive feedback personally, I too have found I do the same thing. I have worked very hard on this issue, as it is not in my nature to just move on or let things drop and roll off. I have found that in order to improve I need to listen more to feedback, reflect, and then evaluate what can I do differently that may help my boss which in turn can help with the constructive feedback I have received. Sometimes I have found I receive constructive feedback mostly when my boss is stressed or has high demand deadlines. In realizing this, I have taken actions to ask proactively what I can do to help, which in turn has benefited me in learning and improving my communication with my boss.

Peer 2 – I relate to your self-identified area of improvement regarding receiving constructive feedback in the moment. I also tend to dislike receiving constructive feedback "in the moment," but I have learned over time to always remind myself that the person giving that feedback is providing it because they are interested in my personal development.

In past instances where I didn't enjoy constructive feedback, I made it a point to reflect on it later – when I am feeling calm. When I recall and think about constructive feedback when feeling calm, it is easier to be receptive to their suggestions.

Receiving constructive feedback is also easier when the person giving the feedback is a trusted colleague, mentor, or mentee. I have found that when I trust and value the person giving feedback, the negative emotions I may feel "in the moment" from others usually don't occur since I know before the conversation even starts that other person has my best interests in mind.

It's great that you already have a mentor. I highly recommend leveraging them to assist you with identifying your strengths and weaknesses (from their perspective) and then building a development plan with specific goals and a timeline. Your mentor can help hold you accountable to achieving your goals on time, while providing feedback between them.

Peer 3 – It can be an easy reflex to become defensive and view criticism as negative. But by undergoing such evaluations we can better ourselves. Even when one tries to be as objective as possible and still disagrees with an assessment, the feedback is still valuable because it contains information about how actions are being perceived. As perceptions are key to trusted leadership, it is important to be aware of this social context no matter what the intent behind actions is.

There is also some responsibility involved with those offering criticism. Some scholars emphasize the importance of respect-driven relationship building as a precursor for constructive criticism, arguing that without the establishment of respectful interactions a critic may take on the role of an "accuser." Recall the Greek philosopher, Aristotle, in describing the true meaning of criticism as making a judgment for the sake of improvement. These viewpoints highlight the importance of both receiving and offering criticism constructively, and that both actions take place along the two-way street of respect.

Middle Manager D – My assessment shows that I demonstrate a strong commitment to being accountable, act honestly, follow ethical guidelines consistently, communicate transparently, and show respect for others. However, there was a discrepancy between my current leadership profile and the desired profile. An area that I can improve on is my ability to balance the organizational needs with my own personal priorities, such as putting others' best interests above my own. This shows that it is important to align my leadership approach with the behaviors that I aspire to. I can do this by improving my decision-making through collaboration and building stronger connections with stakeholders.

A challenge that I have in maintaining my ideal leadership profile is remaining adaptable while also staying true to my values. In high pressure situations like the workplace, leading with ethics and transparency can be difficult. Perceptions of trustworthy leadership are usually dependent on the situation and one's individual perspective. This makes it harder to meet the expectations of everyone. To address this, I plan to improve my communication skills by asking for regular feedback from my colleagues and my manager. This would ensure that my leadership style reflects my own values while also aligning with the needs of the organization.

Having a mentor is a key component to personal and professional growth. I plan to use my manager as a mentor to help guide my improvement efforts. A mentor is someone who embodies trustworthy leadership principles. My manager has years of professional experience and has a better understanding of our organizational culture, which would be useful in helping me navigate challenges and improve my leadership skills. My mentor can also offer valuable insights on how to make better decisions and provide feedback on my progress. Reflecting on my actions and using insights from my mentor would help to bridge the gap between where I am now and where I want to be as a leader.

Peer 1 – It would not be practical for organizational leaders to be overly rigid with their viewpoints as workplace situations undergo changes. On the other hand, there are certain values that each of us have that we would like to think of as being uncompromisable. How can the two concepts be balanced? How does one know which viewpoint should be reconsidered and which one should not? In anticipation of change, it is important to spend some time contemplating what is important and develop contingencies about how to respond to possible scenarios. This helps to distinguish what really is important to us based on logic and reasoning, rather than letting emotions or gut reactions guide our choices.

Conclusion

This chapter has practical implications with respect to leadership development. It encourages senior executives and middle managers to build and preserve trust in and around the workplace as a strategic value. Further, it motivates leaders to undertake a journey of self-assessment to discover their strengths and weaknesses as they relate to the dimensions of trustworthiness while being true to themselves and others (Belasen & Belasen, 2025).

Trustworthy leaders are aware of their vulnerabilities and have the humility to defer to experts or delegate responsibilities to competent individuals and teams. Integrating vulnerabilities into the range of leader's behavior increases transparency and heightened credibility that not only enhances leadership attributes of honesty and accountability but also encourages followers to work with leaders who are humble.

Self-aware leaders reflect on their personal strengths and weaknesses, are sensitive to how others perceive their words and actions, and act on feedback to take corrective steps to remedy their weaknesses so they can lead more effectively (Roberts et al., 2005). Self-awareness leads to personal control and growth that helps executives and managers play to their personal strengths when guiding individuals and teams to pursue targeted outcomes.

To strengthen the alignment between actual behaviors and expectations from others (e.g., executives, peers, direct reports), assessments can be used periodically to determine how well leaders hone their trustworthiness traits and behavioral skills. As the section on middle managers' reflections reveals, a good way to obtain 270-degree feedback (i.e., supervisors, peers, and employees) is to use the same survey scale to get a sense of how others perceive the trustworthiness of middle managers. Doing so would reveal important focused areas for self-improvement, yielding a better alignment between the leader's self-perceptions and perceptions of trustworthiness by others. Self-assessment tools are valuable for development, providing important clues into personal strengths, weaknesses, and areas for improvement. As will be elaborated in upcoming chapters 4 and 9, assessments from others help increase your awareness and guide your targeted growth. By understanding these aspects, middle managers can set realistic goals, develop improvement plans, monitor their progress, adjust strategies as needed, and celebrate their success.

References

APA. (2023). American Psychological Association's Work in America Survey Workplaces as engines of psychological health and well-being. https://www.apa.org/pubs/reports/work-in-america/2023-workplace-health-well-being#:~:text=Workplace%20stress%20also%20remains%20at,emotional%20exhaustion%20(31%25).

Atir, S. & Dunning, D. (2024). Research: Competent leaders know the limits of their expertise. *Harvard Business Review*. https://hbr.org/2024/09/research-competent-leaders-know-the-limits-of-their-expertise.

Barrett, H., & Kemp, A. (2024). Disruptive change is hitting leaders and managers hardest. *Gallup*, May 23. https://www.gallup.com/workplace/645152/disruptive-change-hitting-leaders-managers-hardest.aspx.

Belasen, A. T. & Belasen, A. R. (2017). Strengthening the middle line: Overcoming motivational gaps, supporting promising managers, Best Paper, *Proceedings of the Seventy-Seventh Annual Meeting of the Academy of Management*. Online ISSN: 2151–6561. https://doi.org/10.5465/AMBPP.2017.7.

Belasen, A. T. & Belasen, A. R. (2019). The strategic value of integrated corporate communication: Functions, social media, stakeholders. *International Journal of Strategic Communication*, 13(4). https://doi.org/10.1080/1553118X.2019.1661842.

Belasen, A. T. & Belasen, A. R. (2025). Signaling trust during disruptions: Perceived gender differences in trustworthy leadership traits. *Gender in Management: An International Journal*. https://doi.org/10.1108/GM-04-2024-0187.

Belasen, A. T. & Eisenberg, B. (2023). Building trust for better crisis communication: Lessons for leadership development. Chapter 7 in Nicole Pfeffermann & Monika Schaller (Eds.), *New*

Leadership Communication - Inspire Your Horizon, pp. 93–110, Switzerland: Springer. https://doi.org/10.1007/978-3-031-34314-8_7.

Belasen, A. & Rufer, R. (2013). Innovation communication for effective inter-professional collaboration: A stakeholder perspective. In Nicole Pfeffermann, Tim Minshall, & Letizia Mortara (Eds.), *Strategy and Communication for Innovation*, 2nd edition, pp. 227–240, Germany: Springer.

Covey, S. M. R. (2008). *The Speed of Trust*. Simon & Schuster.

DDI. (2025). Leadership trust crisis. https://www.ddiworld.com/research/global-leadership-forecast2025#:~:text=Leadership%20credibility%20is%20eroding%2C%20with,pipelines%2C%20and%20undermines%20organizational%20performance.

DDI. (2023). 7 leadership behaviors to build trust. https://www.ddiworld.com/blog/build-trust-in-the-workplace.

Fast Company. (2024). Here's what happens when employees don't trust their leadership, November 7. https://www.fastcompany.com/91222315/heres-what-happens-when-employees-dont-trust-their-leadership.

Gardner, W., Avolio, B., Luthans, F., May, D., & Walumbwa, F. (2005). Can you see the real me? A self-based model of authentic leader and follower development. *The Leadership Quarterly*, 16(3), 343–372.

Herne, K., Lappalainen, O., Setälä, M. *et al.* (2022). Accountability as a warrant for trust: An experiment on sanctions and justifications in a trust game. *Theory Decision*, 93, 615–648 https://doi.org/10.1007/s11238-021-09864-7.

Oreg, S., Bartunek, J. M., Lee, G., & Do, B. (2018). An affect-based model of recipients' responses to organizational change events. *The Academy of Management Review*, 43(1), 65–86. https://doi.org/10.5465/amr.2014.0335.

Roberts, L., Spreitzer, G. M., Dutton, J. E., Quinn, R. E., Heaphy, E., & Barker, B. (2005). How to play to your strengths. *Harvard Business Review*, 83(1), 75–80.

Saunders, M. N., Dietz, G., & Thornhill, A. (2014). Trust and distrust: Polar opposites, or independent but co-existing? *Human Relations*, 67(6), 639–665. https://doi.org/10.1177/0018726713500831.

SHRM. (2023). SHRM Research: Work is negatively impacting employees' mental health, May 1. https://www.shrm.org/topics-tools/news/benefits-compensation/shrm-research-work-negatively-impacting-employees-mental-health.

SHRM. (2024). Here's how bad burnout has become at work, April 30. https://www.shrm.org/topics-tools/news/inclusion-diversity/burnout-shrm-research-2024#:~:text=Workers%20who%20feel%20burned%20out,a%20greater%20sense%20of%20purpose.

WHO. (2024). Mental health at work, September 2. https://www.who.int/news-room/fact-sheets/detail/mental-health-at-work.

Zak, P. J. (2017). Trust factor: The science of creating high-performance companies. *AMACOM.*

Chapter 4

Promoting Transparency in the Workplace

DOI: 10.4324/9781003608028-4

Introduction

Great leaders earn the public trust of followers by communicating with clarity, focus, transparency, and compassion. Without transparency, the public may sense deception, which can reduce the credibility of the leader. In the wake of the COVID-19 pandemic, Singapore's political leadership delivered a series of informative and medically accurate communications and succeeded in conveying clear and trustworthy advice to the public consistent with the best available public health information. The main takeaway was cohesive messaging and dissemination of relevant information matter. Furthermore, transparent messaging that health and economic risks were asymmetrically distributed also facilitated the process of confidence-building, enhanced leadership credibility, and boosted public trust.

Middle managers play a critical role in the flow of communication across hierarchical and functional lines of the organization, relaying relevant information accurately and openly from senior executives to frontline leaders and teams, essential for linking operations, coordinating tasks, and building a culture of trust. Transparency is crucial for establishing credibility as middle managers perform a communication pathway role linking senior executives and employees who interact directly with customers or clients.

Accurate, open, and timely exchanges of both upward and downward communication ensure that everyone is on board with tasks and activities consistent with the mission and goals of the organization. By sharing relevant information up and down the chain of command and openly discussing concerns, middle managers encourage employee engagement and facilitate change. Transparent communication promotes a coordinated effort across key interfaces, boosting project integrity, facilitating interactions, and preventing unnecessary confusion or disruptions. When communication is transparent and honest it motivates people to act cohesively in pursuing common goals and priorities or meeting expectations.

A deficiency in transparency occurs when executives and managers attempt to act with a sense of urgency rather than strategy (Belasen & Belasen, 2025). Many times, they are too inwardly focused, paying disproportionate attention to operational and financial objectives while deliberately withholding information or ignoring the need of others to know what's going on. Failing to communicate important decisions to direct reports or neglecting to keep employees informed about crucial updates or developments that directly impact their work may frustrate employees leading to low morale and affecting productivity among team members.

If left unaddressed, a lack of transparency can create ripple effects throughout the organization, tarnishing the credibility of leadership, eroding the culture, and affecting the overall performance of the organization. This ripple effect can lead to further frustration, mistrust, decreased morale, and ultimately, to a breakdown in the flow of organizational communication. Refocusing leaders' behaviors on transparent communication and using messaging strategies that enhance honesty, credibility, and accountability within the organization promotes the psychological safety of employees and fosters a sense of loyalty and commitment to the strategic goals of the organization.

This chapter begins by describing aspects of encoding/decoding in he communication process along with potential barriers to communication and ways to improve interpersonal communication. The second section shifts the discussion to the organizational level including downward, upward, lateral, diagonal, and external communications. The third and fourth sections cover communication gaps between senior executives and middle managers and the importance of articulaing consistent messaging strategies.

The rest of the chapter includes tools and frameworks for building trust in communication, prioritizing transparency, ensuring consistency in actions and words by delivering on promises, admitting mistakes, using reflective listening, showing empathy and mutual respect, and openly asking for and acting on feedback.

The Process of Communication

Communication involves the exchange of targeted messages between senders and receivers. Receivers are internal and external target audiences that may include managers, employees, and external stakeholders. When receivers require senders to provide more information or to clarify some aspects of the message (e.g., when employees ask their manager to clarify the purpose of new missives), they also act as senders. Thus, an overlap in communication roles between senders and receivers occurs in an exchange in which both sides have opportunities to clarify, extend, revise, reinforce, or challenge the intent of the message.

The communication process is contextual and interactive (Figure 4.1), allowing both sides to adjust the communication, make necessary corrections, and align their expectations. The exchange of information involves encoding and decoding. Encoding refers to the process of transforming a thought or message verbally and nonverbally so the receiver can

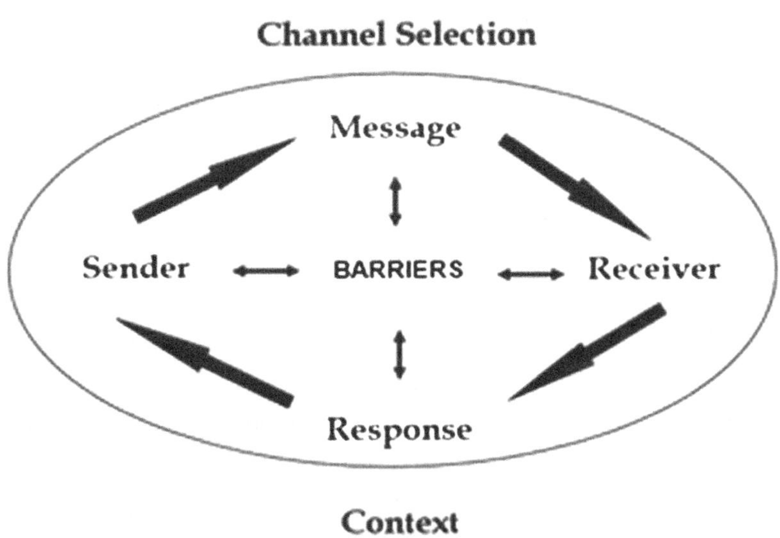

Figure 4.1 The Communication Process

understand it. And decoding is the interpretation of the message by the receiver. When the sender and receiver agree on the content, the communication becomes meaningful.

Contextual factors include the interests, motives, and values of the communicators. Feedback loops and simultaneous exchanges between multiple players (e.g., executives, managers, and employees) make the communication process both dynamic and circular. The process of communication through giving and receiving feedback allows the parties to engage in a meaningful exchange that also considers the objectives of both sides.

An effective flow of communication occurs when senders and receivers are engaged in a meaningful exchange of feedback. However, the exchange is often filtered through "noises" or barriers that need to be dealt with or overcome before a meaningful outcome could be obtained. Examples of barriers that might hinder the achievement of acceptable outcomes are hidden motives, gaps in expectations, incompatible values, cultural differences, mistrust, or lack of credibility. Other barriers may include language and the use of complex metaphors, intended or unintended ambiguity, misinterpretations, and misunderstandings.

The challenge for communicators is to conduct the exchange of communication constructively and persuasively until a mutual understanding is established. When encoding (senders' expressions of thoughts) and decoding (receivers' interpretation of messages) are in sync, the communication process is effective.

The key is to compose the appropriate message by figuring out "what" are the objectives of the communication, "who" is the target, and "how" (i.e., verbal, visual) and "when" the message should be delivered. The selection of suitable channels is just as important. A concerned frontline supervisor may request a middle manager, for example, to compose a formal written report that accurately addresses facts and details of a compliance procedure in question. A senior executive may require a middle manager to present key operational issues and clarify or respond to questions orally.

Face-to-face communication is often the preferred medium for frontline employees who use the opportunity to ask questions and receive feedback about tasks or projects more quickly and thoroughly than via electronic communication. It is also important to remember that some people learn better through oral instruction and others through written or visual instruction and, therefore, it is essential that both types of communication be used to reach all members of a team. Even if messages are originally sent digitally, they could be reinforced with follow up face-to-face communications.

The main challenge is to recognize the need to gain the trust and mutual respect of the parties to communication. Trust is built when the communicators migrate toward each other with reciprocal exchanges that are positive and symmetrical and when the messages are composed clearly and coherently. Thus, in selecting the right channel of communication, the goal is to reduce the "noise," improve the trusting relationship between the parties to the communication, enhance credibility in the engagement, and ultimately gain the attention of the target audience, or receivers.

Sometimes, however, the exchange is complicated by "role ambiguity," such as when middle managers face the challenge of communicating through "dual roles." This occurs when they simultaneously act as a conduit between senior executives, conveying their directives to frontline operators, while also representing the needs and concerns of their teams back to executives, often requiring them to navigate potentially conflicting priorities and messages. This tension requires middle managers to possess sophisticated communication skills and have the knack to facilitate interactions (Belasen & Belasen, 2017).

Studies show that middle managers operate within the realm of difficult policies, procedures, and guidelines; and without consistent top-down communication, are often left unsure of what is required of them. Rarely do we see that commitment to the overall goals or strategies is problematic for middle managers. Instead, their challenge often involves operating with incomplete information, or untimely communication and resources needed to support their work.

The Paradox of Communication

One of the authors of this book was invited as a consultant by a service organization to conduct a communication assessment across their administrative levels. The CEO's office received the results of the survey's feedback showing that over 75% of the employees feel that their bosses discourage them from coming by to discuss problems or get advice.

A second issue involved self-serving perceptions with different hierarchical levels seeing their own communication methods as prompt and successful, while simultaneously dismissing the communication practices of other levels as inadequate, often leading to confusion and unnecessary tension that hamper coordination (see Table 4.1).

A third issue was the failure of management to understand how to use the informal networks of communication to get things done. In the next section, we will focus on the communication gap between senior executives and middle managers.

Executives might believe their communication is strategic and concise, while criticizing middle managers for not "thinking big picture." Meanwhile, middle managers complain that senior executives do not sufficiently listen to their concerns, provide timely feedback, understand the details of complex tasks, limit their ability to act on pressing issues, and

Table 4.1 How Often Decisions Are Communicated Down The Chain

	Frequently (you down the chain)	*Sometimes (you down the chain)*	*Seldom (you down the chain)*	*Never (you down the chain)*
Senior executives	50 (70)	30 (20)	10 (5)	10 (5)
Middle managers	10 (80)	20 (15)	45 (5)	25 (0)
Frontline supervisors	25 (90)	30 (5)	40 (5)	5 (0)

Source: Belasen, A.T. & Belasen, A.R. (2017). "Strengthening the Middle Line."

adequately acknowledge their contributions when implementing strategies.

Figure 4.2 illustrates the perceived communication gap between middle managers and senior executives across four dimensions. Relational communication involves social interactions and highlights the significance of establishing reciprocal trust, honesty, empathy, and mutual respect. Promotional communication relates to performance credibility and strategies to meet organizational objectives. Transformational communication deals with disruptions, is insightful, mind-stretching, and visionary. Hierarchical communications are practical and informative and focus on accountability, compliance, and control (Belasen & Frank, 2010).

While middle managers (outer chart) rate their behaviors as highly effective across the dimensions of communication, executives rated them as less effective (inner chart) in all dimensions. This leaves middle managers feeling undervalued and unable to effectively bridge the performance (and

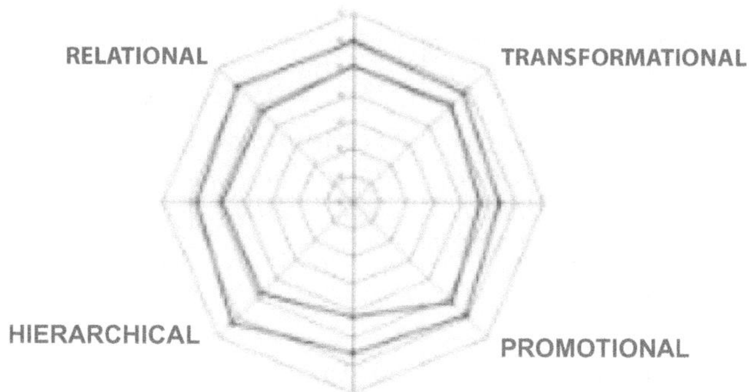

Figure 4.2 Perceptual Gap Between Middle Managers and Senior Executives

communication!) gap between the company's strategic goals and the day-to-day operations, potentially leading to a lack of alignment and difficulty translating the vision into tangible results.

Important decisions that directly improve the effectiveness of operations or streamline work processes, are often communicated down the chain more formally and frequently to ensure transparency and alignment across the organization. An interesting question is how often senior executives communicate decisions as soon as possible after they are made. Decisions can be communicated through a combination of channels like direct meetings, emails, or phone, depending on the importance and urgency of the decision. As Table 4.1 shows, senior executives say that 90% of the time they communicate important changes or new decisions downward either frequently or sometimes.

Middle managers, on the other hand, claim that executives often fail to inform them of important decisions in a timely manner. According to the middle managers, senior executives communicate important changes or new decisions either frequently or sometimes only 30% of the time. Interestingly, middle managers say that they communicate updates and new information to frontline supervisors 95% of the time, while frontline supervisors claim that the percentage of getting communications from middle managers either frequently or sometimes is only 55% of the time.

The contradictory findings point to a paradox of communication across hierarchical levels in which each level perceives the downward flow of communication as highly effective while lower levels perceive the communication to be seemingly ineffective. A common cause is the inherent power dynamics within a hierarchy that often create barriers to effective and transparent communication, leading to information being filtered, withheld, or distorted as it moves up or down the chain of command. Paradoxically, the very administrative structure that is designed to facilitate the flow of communication also hinders the effectiveness of communication.

Managers at all levels might not hold regular meetings, fail to actively listen to employee concerns, or do not provide clear instructions when sharing information. These poor communication practices and the lack of transparency create unnecessary bottlenecks or communication lags leading to inefficiencies, missed opportunities, and a sense of distrust and uncertainty among employees.

Sometimes the reason may involve misperception or overconfidence when managers assume that employees already have access to information without verifying their understanding. They might also prioritize urgent matters over taking the time to fully inform employees, leading to communication gaps. A lack of transparent communication channels often triggers grapevine communication when employees resort to gossiping and informal networks to gather information or hear about important updates, further complicating relationships.

Promoting a culture of trust, encouraging transparency, and creating mechanisms for employees to raise concerns and discuss common issues without fear of retribution are key recommendations to address this paradox. Understanding the purpose and direction of organizational communication, using empathic communication and active listening to receive feedback from lower levels, and demonstrating honest interest in their aspirations and goals are important means for improving transparency in upward and downward communication (Belasen & Eisenberg, 2023).

Directions of Communication

Communication in an organization flows downward, upward, laterally, diagonally, and externally. Downward communication flows from the top-down and is used by leaders and managers to assign tasks and responsibilities, provide clarifications about strategies and policies, ensures that everyone is working in sync with organizational goals, and points out problems that need to be addressed. Downward communication that travels through multiple levels of hierarchy in an organization, can potentially become distorted, delayed, or misinterpreted, leading to a loss of clarity and to information underload, potentially impacting the effectiveness of the message reaching the intended recipients at lower levels.

The more administrative layers involved, the higher the probability of misinterpretations and misunderstandings. Traveling through multiple layers can significantly increase the time it takes for information to reach its intended target, causing bottlenecks and risking implementation issues that require immediate attention.

Diagonal communication acts as a great mitigator by allowing individuals from different departments and hierarchical levels to directly communicate with each other, thus increasing the efficiency of cross-functional collaboration within an organization, fostering better teamwork and faster problem-solving. By enabling communication across departments, it skips unnecessary layers and facilitates information sharing between individuals who might not normally interact. This not only builds trusting relationships but also offers insights into coordination challenges (e.g., logistical delays, safety management, quality control, cybersecurity) and where synergies can be explored for mutual benefit, creating win–win outcomes for the organization.

Upward communication flows bottom-up, allowing employees to voice their opinions and provide perspectives on various aspects of operations, work processes, policies, and projects, or share ideas and suggestions directly with managers or higher-ups. It gives employees a platform to respond to follow-up inquiries, provide updates and progress reports, and relay issues and problems that require further attention from managers.

When downward and upward communications are clear and transparent, employees feel appreciated and work with elevated sense of confidence. However, upward communications are often hindered by a lack of transparency, information filtering (where employees' messages are altered by supervisors before reaching higher management), or distortion when employees modify the narratives to please their manager, causing important details to be omitted or distorted when they reach higher levels.

Other reasons that reduce the effectiveness of upward communication include hesitation to report concerns, reluctance to share negative information due to fear of repercussions like job security or negative performance evaluations, potential delays in reporting issues, lack of clarity due to differing experiences between levels, and a possibility of bypassing immediate supervisors to reach higher management, potentially leading to tensions.

Upward communication can be improved by prioritizing transparent communication, giving and receiving feedback, promoting a culture of openness and mutual respect, ensuring a safe workplace climate, encouraging participation and creating opportunities for employees to get together and talk openly. In business, the use of MBO (management by objectives) involves managers and employees working together to set and achieve specific goals. In healthcare, leadership rounding is an example of a process where leaders connect with care teams, staff, and patients to have meaningful conversations to improve services and build relationships.

In addition to creating a workplace culture where employees feel comfortable sharing their ideas and concerns, organizations rely on horizontal communication to help synchronize activities and tasks between individuals or departments at the same hierarchical level. Horizontal communication helps validate the flow of information between adjacent departments and fellow employees, enabling better teamwork and sharing among peers by exchanging information across different functions or teams. Different groups within the same hierarchical level can discuss matters that are critical to achieving their goals and address common issues that arise in real time thus alleviating the inefficiencies inherent in upward communications.

The role of external communication is to build and maintain a positive public image of an organization by disseminating information about financial goals and strategies, reliability, safety, and quality of service with consumers, regulators, investors, and the public. External messaging helps the organization position itself within the industry, create brand awareness, promote performance credibility, and enhance its reputation.

With open access to multiple channels of communication, consumers are becoming major players in the mass consumption of information and in the creation and distribution of information. Faster, immediate, and multi-directional communications spread messages beyond their targeted audiences, making it more difficult to trace attitudes or changes or monitor their direction and potential impact. It is therefore vital for executives and middle managers to create dialogues with useful information to all publics, use conversational forms of communication, generate return visits to the company's website with an easy navigation interface, and provide regular updates (Belasen & Luber, 2017).

Messaging strategies aimed at regulators focus on transparency and monitoring or enforcing compliance and implementation of policies and standard operating procedures. Middle managers often are responsible for communications systems involving dissemination and compliance as well as informing organizational members about issues and policies with broad regulatory implications. They identify strategies to engage members in public policy input, lobby campaigns, and government affairs. The goal is to enhance transparency and accountability by adhering to laws and regulations and by providing accurate information about the organization.

Promoting effective communication with shareholders provides direct financial benefits for publicly owned companies. Trusting relationships between staff and security analysts and the financial community are important for effective communication of financial performance and goals. Institutional investors and analysts receive companies' communications regularly, which help them evaluate those companies' earnings potential as well as the companies' intentions to realize their potential and attain short- and long-term goals. Many companies also distribute financial reports and analyses as well as discuss financial statements and answer shareowners' queries and concerns via webinars and videoconferencing, making investment strategy a cocreation process.

Tailoring message strategies to specific stakeholders as well as detecting the tone of the messages helps executives avoid second-guessing objectives and needs and, instead, focuses their attention on messages that are consistent with the expectations of stakeholders (Belasen & Belasen, 2019). For example, addressing shareowners and investors requires insightful communication that projects energy and credibility, a strong belief in the company's future and growth potential, and a general sense of direction anchored in the vision. Addressing regulators, on the other hand, requires a different tone and style – a communication strategy that presents data both credibly and reliably.

While a company's representatives might draw on success stories to highlight the legality and ethical adherence of codes and standards imposed by regulators, they also use messages that are confirming and validating. Middle managers, for example, may use storytelling and symbols along with powerful media to present innovative organizational pursuits in a rich, colorful way that connects the audience on impact. How they respond to situations and present themselves can be profoundly influential and can affect the perception of the organization as trustworthy.

MANAGING UP, DOWN, SIDEWAYS, AND OUT

Navigating the intricate maze of managing in multiple directions can undoubtedly feel overwhelming at times. However, the dividends of such a comprehensive approach are both tangible and rewarding. By prioritizing enhanced communication, organizations stand to gain significantly. This includes the optimization of workflow, resulting in increased efficiency. A workforce that feels connected, heard, and understood translates into higher levels of engagement and dedication. Additionally, when communication with external entities is nurtured and valued, it solidifies stronger, more lasting relationships. The environment created by such holistic management also becomes fertile ground for innovation, fostering a culture that's agile and adaptable to change.

Gone are the days when impressing your boss was the sole ticket to success. Today's multifaceted business environment requires a holistic approach to management communication. By effectively engaging with colleagues, superiors, reports, and external stakeholders, professionals can drive organizational success and carve a path to individual achievement (Laker, 2023).

Messaging Strategies

Leadership is about making employees feel safe, creating an atmosphere that supports innovation and that integrates safety messages into daily operations. Leaders must also be transparent. According to Clampitt et al. (2000), executives tend to gravitate toward less effective forms of communication such as "spray & pray" (abundant communication) or "withhold & uphold" (limited communication). In fact, overcommunicating can be as destructive as under-communicating.

Too much communication can cause confusion, misunderstandings, loss of productivity, and can overwhelm those on the receiving end. Withholding communication, on the other hand, can lead to distrust, confusion, and low morale. Instead, executives should opt for the strategy of "explore & underscore" with an articulation of a few vital messages linked to organizational outcomes, while actively listening to potential problems.

An important question is how managers select the right approach, which emphasizes style over content, to communicate different tasks and goals. This section focuses on the value of aligning message orientations to the type of stakeholders that leaders engage in their daily operations. These messages are designed to match the purpose, medium, focus, and target audience (Table 4.2).

Table 4.2 Messaging Approaches

	Relational	*Transformational*	*Hierarchical*	*Promotional*
Objective is to…	Establish trust and transparency, rapport, confidence, and commitment	Inspire the audience to think creatively	Provide clear directions to receivers, establish accountability	Instigate suggestions, innovative, establish credibility
Messaging tone is…	Conversational, authentically honest, emphatic, respectful	Visionary, charismatic, idealized, colorful, oral delivery	Formal, evaluative, assertive, concrete, instructive	Insightful, evidence-based, urgent
Focus is…	Person-centered	Contextual	Manager-centric	Persuasive
Intended targets include	Employees, peers	Consumers, investors	Employees, regulators	Executives, Partners, stakeholders
Example	Leadership rounding, dialogue, active listening, supportive, giving and receiving feedback	CEO speech, bombastic, metaphors, symbols, rhetorical, communicating vision	documents, lists, tables, audit reports policy statements, procedural specifications, written documents, memos, directives	presentations to senior executives, press releases, quarterly results, financial reports

Source: Adapted from Belasen, A. (2008). The Theory and Practice of Corporate Communication.

Discovering your Strengths and Weaknesses

Having a strong understanding of the frequency (amount of content), direction (who the message is directed to), and tenacity of the message (impact of the message or influence of the source of the message) can help mitigate communication roadblocks as well as clarify leadership expectations. When the lines of communication are clear and the messages reach their target audiences with the right approach, the consistency of communication increases. This also helps reduce miscommunications and the potential for conflict between senders and receivers.

Knowing in advance what managers communicate, as well as detecting the tone of the messages, should also help middle managers avoid second guessing the expectations of senior executives (Belasen & Frank, 2010).

For each statement in Table 4.3, indicate the behavior that you will most likely use. You will have two responses: one that describes the messages as they are now; the second that describes messages as they should be (preferred). These responses will be the same if the message is exactly as you think it should be for the situation.

In Figure 4.3, the manager seems to place more weight on promotional and hierarchical approaches than on transformational and relational, limiting communication to formal logic, discipline, and credibility. This manager's profile, on the other hand, shows a clear gap with a preference for shifting more toward transformational and relational approaches.

The gap between the two charts in Figure 4.3 represents opportunities for self-improvement. When employees, peers, supervisors, or even external stakeholders provide their inputs, this framework can become a powerful tool for guiding improvement efforts based on expectations from others. When communication strategies are aligned with effective emotional intelligence (EI) skills, they also enhance the ability to listen

Table 4.3 Assessment: Message Orientations

Frequency level – Likert 7 point *1 – Never* *2 – Rarely, in less than 10% of the chances when I could have* *3 – Occasionally, in about 30% of the chances when I could have* *4 – Sometimes, in about 50% of the chances when I could have* *5 – Frequently, in about 70% of the chances when I could have* *6 – Usually, in about 90% of the chances I could have* *7 – Every time*	**Actual**	**Preferred**
When I communicate new directions, I make sure that I am discerning, and perceptive of the receivers' reactions [**aware**]		
When asked for my opinion, the tone of my messages is forceful and prevailing [**emphatic**]		
I inspire peers or team members with messages that are mind stretching and visionary [**insightful**]		
I encourage communications that are creative and original [**innovative**]		
My messages are interesting and stimulating [**engaging**]		
I am conclusive and decisive when I communicate goals to team members [**action oriented**]		
I make big efforts to use realistic and informative messages [**practical**]		
My statements and messages are focused and logical [**organized**]		
I use rigor and consistency in communicating with peers [**precise**]		
I make sure that my messages are technically correct [**accurate**]		
I use credible and believable communications with peers and team members [**plausible**]		
My communication with others is open and candid [**honest**]		

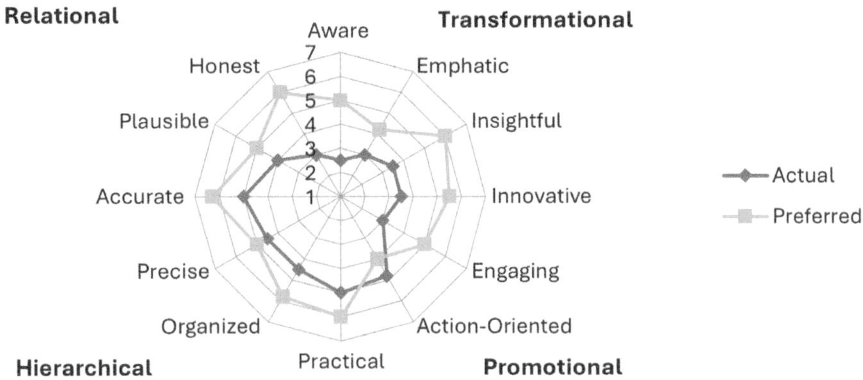

Figure 4.3 Actual and Preferred Message Orientations

actively and empathize with others, as well as improve the quality of interpersonal relationships.

Emotional Intelligence (EI)

Goffee and Jones in *Why Should Anyone Be Led by You?* (2000) suggest that emotionally intelligent (EI) leaders share four common qualities: they understand their weaknesses, rely heavily on intuition to display clear commitment to decisions and actions, manage employees with tough empathy, and selectively reveal their differences. Revealing personal differences requires a strong sense of personal integrity and moral courage. Verbalizing personal vulnerabilities demonstrates humility and honesty. It conveys humility and self-confidence. When a leader admits to weaknesses, it creates trust and opportunities for collaboration and joint accountability.

The ability to collect and interpret relevant information requires intuition and analysis. There is an abundant amount of information that reaches middle managers and senior executives from multiple directions, creating complexity. Leaders leverage intuition to navigate complexity by limiting the scope of the problems or by prioritizing events with greater impact, which can then be analyzed in a logical way. The reverse is true, too. A rational analysis may reveal a few options good enough to solve the problems, and intuition is then used to single out the right one.

Practicing tough empathy, however, requires the leader to make unpopular decisions. It prevents followers from becoming too complacent by eliciting their opinions and suggestions. Effective EI leaders use their differences to keep social distance but, at the same time, make sure not to over-differentiate to prevent mistrust.

EI leaders may acknowledge their vulnerabilities, but if a weakness involves incompetence, it may have adverse effects on peers and followers. This is where self-assessment and self-development are important tools for continuous improvement. Assessing your messaging approaches (Table 4.3) and EI skills (Table 4.4) and learning how to adjust your relationships with others demonstrate your moral courage, show that you are transparent and honest with followers and create a collaborative workplace that boosts shared accountability and active listening, incentivizing a culture that values diverse perspectives.

The chart in Figure 4.4 reveals the gaps between current levels of beliefs and attitudes versus desired levels across the five skills of emotional intelligence. Good leaders are aware of their own leadership style and use their learning experience to improve their communication relationships. Knowing your EI strengths and weaknesses helps reduce stress and promote healthy relationships. Improving your EI skills across the five categories will make you a leader with the empathy and communication sensitivity skills to lead teams effectively.

Moving meaningfully from the current EI skills to the desired level requires further training and development. When materialized, strong EI skills help facilitate positive interactions, build mutual trust, and enhance communication and listening skills. One tool to help leverage the benefits of the assessments in Tables 4.3 and 4.4 is the Johari Window.

Table 4.4 Assessing Emotional Intelligence

Frequency Level (Seven-Point Likert 7 Scale)		
Thinking about your attitudes and beliefs when working with teams and individuals, reflect on each statement by indicating the response that best matches your beliefs, first in terms of the actual (i.e., current beliefs, views, behaviors) and then in terms of desired expectations.		
1—Very untrue of what I believe *2—Untrue of what I believe* *3—Somewhat untrue of what I believe* *4—Neutral* *5—Somewhat true of what I believe* *6—True of what I believe* *7—Very true of what I believe*		
Emotional intelligence skills	**Actual**	**Desired**
Self-awareness		
I recognize immediately when I am short-tempered		
I am aware when I am happy		
I know when I feel stressed out		
I can tell when I am emotional		
I am aware when I feel anxious		
I can detect my own anger		
AVERAGE		
Self-regulation		
I can let go of my anger when someone hurts my feelings		
I can control my mood		

(Continued)

Table 4.4 (Continued) Assessing Emotional Intelligence

Emotional intelligence skills	Actual	Desired
I do not hold a grudge when someone annoys me		
I can consciously alter my frame of mind		
I do not let stressful situations overcome me		
I can separate work stressors from my life		
AVERAGE		
Motivation		
I am internally motivated to accomplish challenging tasks		
I am motivated complete my work on time		
I always meet my personal goals		
I set my priorities and manage my time productively		
I can challenge myself to accomplish difficult tasks		
I feel motivated when challenged		
AVERAGE		
Empathy		
I can understand the other person's perspectives		
I can empathize with others		
I can tell if someone is upset with me		
I can understand if I am being unreasonable		
I can understand the effects of my decisions on others		
I can see things from others' point of view.		

(*Continued*)

Table 4.4 (Continued) Assessing Emotional Intelligence

Emotional intelligence skills	Actual	Desired
AVERAGE		
Social		
I am a good listener when others communicate with me		
I do not interrupt others' conversations		
I enjoy interacting with others		
I am comfortable working with individuals and teams		
I am good at reconciling differences with others		
I know how to build respect through trust		
AVERAGE		

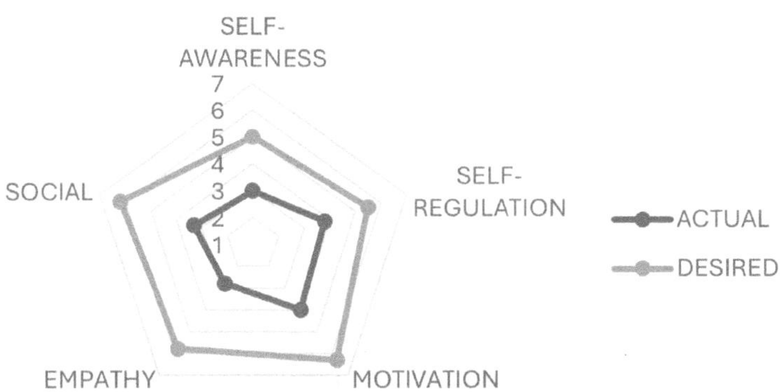

Figure 4.4 Assessing Your EI Skills

The Johari Window

Do people listen to you because of how you sound and what you look like, or do they listen to you because of the value of your ideas, the clarity of your statements, or the incisiveness of your thinking?

Most people believe they are listened to because of the value of their ideas. On the other hand, research shows that most people listen with an attempt to reply (they hear you, which is a biological function) rather than listen to understand (which is an intellectual function)! The actual answer may involve both.

Listeners may be influenced as much by the "how" you say things (nonverbal) as by "what" you say (substance, meaning). Your style of communication may be more obvious to others than you think. The Johari Window (Figure 4.5) can be used by leaders to help create an environment where people are more open and honest, which facilitates better communication.

The Johari Window is a framework for enhancing communication effectiveness based on interpersonal understanding by oneself and others. It facilitates effective conflict resolution for leaders by promoting transparency and understanding of diverse perspectives. The framework encourages empathy and active listening, enabling leaders to identify common ground, reconcile differences, and foster stronger relationships within their teams.

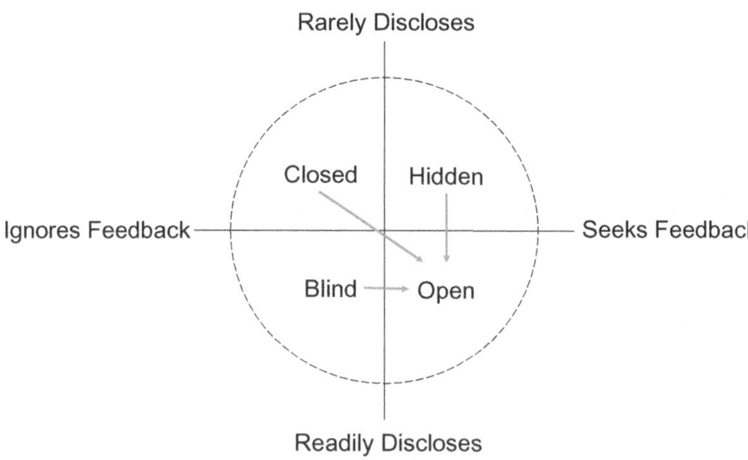

Figure 4.5 The Johari Window

The Open quadrant represents information that is known to the communicator (sender) and is also known to the group (receiver/s). The goal is to expand the open quadrant for everyone involved where effective communication and cooperation take place.

The Blind quadrant includes things that are known about an individual by others but are unknown to the individual (e.g., not making eye contact). Blind spots can be reduced through strong self-awareness skills and empathetic feedback; leaders reduce the blind area.

The Hidden quadrant represents things that an individual knows about himself/herself but keeps hidden from others (e.g., feelings, emotions, important information). Providing feedback and information that is relevant for the group helps reduce misunderstandings and conflicts, improve trusting relationships, and moves attention to the open (window).

The Closed quadrant represents the information gap for all parties involved in communication. Through self-discovery, people can move information from unknown areas to the Hidden or Open areas.

Middle managers in a training program reflect on the following question – Does the Johari Window seem like a good framework for leaders who want to improve communications among team members? Can you think of potential problems a leader might encounter when applying the Johari Window? Here are some answers.

Middle Manager A – "The Johari window model is an excellent way for a leader to improve communications between team members. However, I think there is a danger that the tool may create relationship rifts if not administered carefully. I have witnessed confidential 360-degree feedback tools that expose areas of potential blind spots. I recall a specific incident where a leader wanted to know which of his subordinates gave that feedback so he could 'set them straight.' The tool wasn't intended to set the subordinate straight, it was intended to help the leader understand how people were feeling."

Middle Manager B – "The hidden areas seem like they can be reduced by frequent two-way communication inviting Q&A. The same holds true here, if the presenter can't handle negative feedback and responds negatively, it seems like the trust gets worse instead of better. The hidden area gets bigger instead of smaller."

Middle Manager C – "The bottom line is that the tool seems like a great model to help think about areas for communication improvement. However, the administration of the tool and preparing the receiver on how to receive and use the information is essential. I also think that simultaneous deployment of the tool to an entire team may create a lot of turmoil, especially if the team is experiencing dysfunction. In such a case, maybe it is best for the leader to practice it first."

The Johari Window offers several advantages, including increased self-awareness, improved communication, stronger relationships, better team dynamics, personal development, identification of blind spots, and the ability to understand how others perceive the communicators. This framework enables individuals and teams to work more cooperatively by fostering open and honest feedback loops. By reflecting on how you are perceived by others, you can gain a clearer view of your strengths, weaknesses, and blind spots, leading to personal development and improvement of your communication skills. When team members are comfortable exchanging feedback, it can foster collaboration, trust, and a more transparent and productive work environment.

ADDITIONAL REFLECTIONS

Middle Manager D – I can see how the Johari Window may be effective in improving interpersonal communications, both verbal and non-verbal. Like many of the other communication frameworks, this exercise involves a process of self-discovery and developing a heightened awareness of one's own personality traits. Given the prominence of non-verbal communication, it would not be surprising that there is much context left out of the "open" window. By having an open dialogue, the window can be expanded.

A potential shortcoming when using the Johari Window, I believe, is its dependence on the participants' openness and willingness to accept constructive criticism. Unlike the Myers–Briggs assessment, which can be completed as an individual, the Johari method requires direct peer feedback. Not everyone can accept such criticism well, and I could imagine defensiveness being a reflex for many. Additionally, in a workplace setting, the instinct of many is to hide the authentic self and seek conformity. For these reasons, I believe the Johari Window would be best applied once an appropriate level of trust is established among members of the group.

Middle Manager E – The question of whether individuals are listened to primarily due to the substance of their ideas or the way they present them is complex and multifaceted. Research indicates that both the content of a speaker's message and their delivery style significantly influence listener engagement and comprehension. For instance, clarity of statements and incisiveness of thinking are critical for effective communication; however, nonverbal cues such as tone, facial expressions, and body language can equally impact how messages are received and interpreted by listeners.

This dual influence suggests that while the value of ideas is paramount, the way these ideas are articulated can enhance or detract from their perceived worth. Moreover, the phenomenon of "listening to reply" rather than "listening to understand" highlights a common barrier in effective communication. Many listeners may focus on formulating their responses rather than fully comprehending the speaker's message, which can lead to misunderstandings and a lack of genuine engagement. This tendency underscores the importance of fostering an environment conducive to active listening, where individuals are encouraged to process information thoughtfully before responding.

The Johari Window model can be instrumental in this context, as it promotes self-awareness and open communication among team members, thereby enhancing the quality of interactions and reducing the blind spots that often hinder effective dialogue. In practical applications, leaders can utilize the Johari Window to facilitate better communication by encouraging feedback and self-disclosure among team members.

By expanding the "open" quadrant, where mutual understanding exists, leaders can create a more collaborative atmosphere that values both the content of ideas and the manner of their presentation. However, potential challenges may arise, such as resistance to feedback or discomfort with vulnerability, which can inhibit the effectiveness of this model. Leaders must navigate these dynamics carefully to foster an environment where open communication thrives.

In conclusion, effective communication is a nuanced interplay of both the substance of ideas and the style of delivery. While listeners may initially be drawn to the value of what is being said, the way it is conveyed plays a crucial role in ensuring that messages are understood and appreciated. The Johari Window framework offers a valuable tool for enhancing communication, but leaders must be mindful of the potential challenges that can arise in its implementation.

Conclusion

Transparency in managerial communication is important because it builds trust in and around the organization, fosters open dialogue, reduces misunderstandings, and improves problem-solving. Transparency contributes to a positive work climate where trustworthy managers and executives model good behaviors by recognizing gaps in communication and by working to improve their communication approaches and their ability to give and receive timely and constructive feedback.

Importantly, transparency creates a positive working environment by ensuring everyone has access to necessary information and feels empowered to contribute openly.

Transparency in decisions and actions and honesty in disseminating and using information is fundamental to building trust, a vital component of building a culture of trust and reliability.

Clear communication with no hidden agendas and with the ability of individuals to give and receive meaningful feedback minimizes the potential for unnecessary confusion and tension that may arise from predisposed assumptions or lack of information. Knowing your communication strategy (e.g., explore and underscore) during times of disruption and using it effectively can reduce conflict and empower people to engage. Likewise, understanding your communication approach by articulating a messaging strategy tailored to target audiences with the appropriate focus, medium of communication, and style, is clearly linked to organizational success (Belasen & Belasen, 2019).

Notably, actively listening to employees' interpretations and concerns to address potential misunderstandings and obstacles during times of disruption helps to increase transparency and trust in the workplace. Employees who feel informed and valued through transparent communication are more likely to be engaged and committed to their work and interfunctional collaboration becomes more effective and productive.

References

Belasen, A. (2008). *The Theory and Practice of Corporate Communication: A Competing Values Perspective.* Thousand Oaks, CA: SAGE.

Belasen, A. T. & Belasen, A. R. (2017). Strengthening the middle line: Overcoming motivational gaps, supporting promising managers, Best Paper, *Proceedings of the Seventy-Seventh Annual Meeting of the Academy of Management.* Online ISSN: 2151–6561.

Belasen, A. T. & Belasen, A. R. (2019). The strategic value of integrated corporate communication: Functions, social media, stakeholders. *International Journal of Strategic Communication*, 13, 4. https://doi.org/10.1080/1553118X.2019.1661842.

Belasen, A. T. & Belasen, A. R. (2025). Signaling trust during disruptions: Perceived gender differences in trustworthy leadership traits. *Gender in Management: An International Journal.* https://doi.org/10.1108/GM-04-2024-0187.

Belasen, A. T. & Eisenberg, B. (2023). Building trust for better crisis communication: Lessons for leadership development. Chapter 7 in Nicole Pfeffermann & Monika Schaller (Eds.), *New Leadership Communication - Inspire Your Horizon*, pp. 93–110, Switzerland: Springer. https://doi.org/10.1007/978-3-031-34314-8_7.

Belasen, A. & Frank, N. M. (2010). A peek through the lens of the competing values framework: What managers communicate and how. *The Atlantic Journal of Communication*, 18, 280–296.

Belasen, A. & Luber, E. (2017). Innovation implementation: Leading from the middle out. In Nicole Pfeffermann & Julie Gould (Eds.), *Strategy and Communication for Innovation: Integrative Perspectives on Innovation in the Digital Economy*, pp. 229–243, Germany: Springer.

Clampitt, P. G., DeKoch, R. J., & Cashman, T. (2000). A strategy for communicating about uncertainty. *The Academy of Management Executive*, 14(4), 41–57.

Goffee, R., & Jones, G. (2000). Why should anyone be led by you?. *Harvard business review*, *78*(5), 62–198.

Laker, B. (2023). Managing up, down, sideways, and out: The holistic approach to workplace communication. *Forbes*, September 13. https://www.forbes.com/sites/benjaminlaker/2023/09/14/managing-up-down-sideways-and-out-the-holistic-approach-to-workplace-communication/.

Chapter 5

Creating a Culture of Accountability

 DOI: 10.4324/9781003608028-5

Introduction

Accountability starts with leadership and requires clear expectations, trust, and follow-through. It builds a strong culture of compliance and strengthens the cooperation between leaders and followers by reinforcing the need to conform with rules and regulations, adhere to standards, and maintain internal consistency. According to Covey (2008), effective leaders need to model trust not through "blind trust," but rather, "smart trust" with clear expectations, open communication, follow-through, and a firm commitment to upholding high moral principles and guidelines, where everyone consistently prioritizes ethical behavior in their decisions and actions. A strong commitment to strengthening accountability and ethical standards demonstrates the motivation to act with integrity and responsibility in sharing information and performing tasks.

A strong culture of compliance ensures that employees take responsibility for their actions, work collaboratively, and continuously strive for improvement. Accountability mechanisms function as guards and incentives that help manage the risks and rewards in communication relationships (Herne et al., 2022). When these mechanisms are in place, they create opportunities for establishing a culture of teamwork and collaboration.

The first section of this chapter explores the role of leadership in securing accountability through a culture of compliance. The second section focuses on identifying destructive leadership behaviors that negate accountability and ways to avert toxicity. The third section covers aspects of collaborative culture, particularly with respect to teamwork and collaboration. Assessment instruments and strategies for improving teamwork are provided with examples and key takeaways. The fourth section covers the importance of building and sustaining high reliability organizations in which middle managers model accountability.

Holding Leaders Accountable

Trust is shown when expectations for accountability ensure that the behaviors of those who are trusted align with the expectations. Trust is the belief that someone will act in a certain way, while accountability is the obligation or willingness to accept responsibility for one's actions. Joint accountability is typically the result of building a culture of trust where collaboration and teamwork are the foundation for high performance teams.

Examples of accountability at the organizational level include setting clear milestones, tracking results by monitoring performance against targets, following up with constructive feedback, utilizing performance reviews, holding meetings to discuss progress, revising or rescheduling tasks with defined responsibilities, ensuring transparency in decision-making processes, and celebrating and acknowledging achievements.

Middle managers ensure compliance by establishing clear protocols that guide ethical behavior and use communication and conflict resolution methods to ensure that processes and outcomes align with organizational goals. By outlining specific rules and procedures, everyone within the organization knows what is expected of them, reducing the chances for errors and misinterpretations. They implement standardized data input formats to prevent inconsistencies and use validation checks with milestones and metrics to actively monitor progress and measure critical aspects of a business or team performance. These efforts help to identify areas for improvement, streamline business workflows, increase employee engagement, and ultimately ensure peer accountability for results and fairness in performance evaluations.

Metrics are indispensable tools for building a culture of accountability. By creating clear, measurable targets and fostering a transparent work environment, metrics encourage employees to take ownership of their roles and contribute effectively to company success (Bentega.io, 2024).

Middle managers use a consistent accounting method like first-in, first-out (FIFO) for businesses with rapidly changing prices and last-in, first-out (LIFO), for businesses that have perishable goods coming in to analyze inventory and report financial data more accurately across time intervals to eliminate unnecessary gaps and further ensure accountability. They examine and update policies and procedures regularly to keep them current and in line with new goals or expectations, monitor compliance, and address any inconsistencies that may arise, thus ensuring accountability across organizational lines.

At the corporate level, mechanisms include executive risk management practices (Sheedy & Canestrari-Soh, 2023) and adhering to acceptable accounting principles by following a set of established accounting standards and guidelines. These are known as Generally Accepted Accounting Principles (GAAP), which ensure transparency and accountability when preparing and presenting a company's financial statements.

Through the value chain, executives cooperate in setting industry standards, agree on reporting practices, and adhere to regulations and industry-wide benchmarks. They take responsibility for the impact of their operations, including environmental sustainability, financial stability, ethical labor practices, and product safety. By openly sharing information about their industry-wide practices and products, companies' senior executives demonstrate accountability but also project an image of a reliable organization. Moreover, they can leverage social media to engage in collaborative networks, enhance innovation and resilience, and succeed in leading their organizations through disruptions (Garrido-Moreno, 2024).

Organizations are also going through third party, independent audit and certification companies, to ensure compliance with regulatory requirements. When organizations and executives take responsibility for the outcomes of their actions, it enhances credibility and accountability. Other tools include industry-wide advocacy by campaigning or engaging with policymakers to promote legislation and regulations and consumer engagement by communicating efforts to allocate resources to improving ethics, equity, and sustainability, building trust and accountability between businesses, investors, and consumers.

One example is the Sarbanes-Oxley Act of 2002 (SOX), a federal law that requires corporations to improve their financial reporting and record keeping. The act was passed in response to widespread corporate fraud in the late 1990s aimed at protecting investors and the public from accounting fraud, increasing the accuracy of financial reporting, improving corporate governance, and holding senior executives accountable for financial statements.

UNETHICAL BEHAVIOR GOES UNREPORTED

Unethical behavior varies widely in severity, from disparaging a coworker to securities fraud. Overall, nearly one in four US employees (23%) say they have personally seen or have first-hand knowledge of their colleagues or manager demonstrating unethical behavior in the past year. These findings were collected in a nationally representative May 2024 Gallup survey of 21,543 employees.

Increased exposure to ethics violations is a symptom of failing management and an unhealthy organizational culture that hinders employees' ability and desire to show up and perform at work every day.

Employees with first-hand awareness of unethical behavior in their organization are 2.7 times as likely to be actively disengaged and 2.3 times as likely to be burned out as their peers.

Awareness of poor ethical practices may also lead employees to detach from their organization and seek a different opportunity. Employees with first-hand awareness of unethical behavior within their organization are 70% less likely to strongly agree that they are connected to their organization's culture. These employees are also 45% more likely to be watching for or actively seeking another job (Kemp, 2024).

When leaders experience a deficiency in accountability, it is often marked by a tendency to shoot from the hip, resulting in making solo decisions without the benefit of input from affected employees or external stakeholders. Executives who project higher levels of accountability know how to resist the temptation to make decisions too hastily, even when the urgent pressures of the moment may push them into doing so.

Unless the problem is extremely urgent and a decision must be made on the spot, leaders should take the time to reflect before making a choice: Is there updated information to support the decision? What is missing? What don't we know? What is the timeline for deciding? Who has the most accurate data? Who else is involved? What are the risks of ignoring the problem? What are the opportunity costs of ignoring the problem or pursuing other solutions? By taking time to reflect, executives avoid the tendency to unilaterally follow the dominant decision or make choices based on intuition rather than logic. They can gather information, solicit suggestions, identify options, and weigh potential consequences to affected stakeholders more systematically, leading to better outcomes.

Identifying and Curbing Destructive Behaviors

Senior executives and middle managers who fail to acknowledge their limitations often tend to think in binary terms and develop strong biases toward what works and what does not work. These biases are then translated into values that permeate their decisions and behaviors. Gradually, these values become deeply held beliefs, ingrained communication styles, and stereotyped behaviors that are repeated. Trapped by their dysfunctional styles and unable to explore or employ positive traits or behaviors, these leaders succumb to continuing their behaviors as usual, avoiding any signals of wrongdoing or lack of accountability.

Unaware of their "blind spots," or the behavioral and perceptual tendencies known to others but unknown to them, these leaders resort to withholding valuable information from employees or to creating dependence by assigning skilled employees to less important roles. Lacking personal integrity, they focus on self-interest and personal gains, as opposed to the collective benefits of organizational members and stakeholders. Often perceived as destructive leaders (Belasen, 2016), they typically operate from the top of the pyramid and commonly share five important characteristics:

- **Personal appeal** – These individuals are influential orators and masters of public speaking that get followers to identify their values and beliefs with those of the leader. When followers accept the values of leaders unconditionally without questioning their motives or moral reasoning, leaders can structure their attitudes and shape their thinking quickly and effectively. Followers internalize the values and goals of these leaders and model their behaviors accordingly, in effect becoming indoctrinated.
- **Abuse of power** – Once these leaders secure dependence of others on them, they use power and control

as important levers to continuously overcome objections or eliminate opponents. They resort to Machiavellian behavior placing political expediency above morality to augment their power and use it for personal gain and self-promotion. More importantly, they consolidate their centralized authority using fear and intimidation tactics which also fuel paranoia and impulsive decision making.

- **Self-centeredness –** Destructive leaders view themselves as the "face" of the group and as superior to the others; therefore, what benefits the leader, benefits the group, because the leader owns the group. These leaders are self-absorbed with an inflated sense of their value, excessively preoccupied with their personal adequacy, attributes, self-importance, and goals.
- **Damaging views –** They promote a worldview saturated with tensions, conflicts, and instability, creating dependence of others on them for interpretation and comfort, further strengthening their dominance.
- **Fear and intimidation –** These leaders will often communicate with group members through rhetoric rich with metaphors and messages containing images of hate or violence. This is accomplished by promoting the superiority and solidarity of the leader-centric primary group and by devaluing outsiders and rivals. Group members are made to feel as if they are under attack by their rivals and that the only way to survive is through their continued blind loyalty to the leader, providing the leader with unconditional support.

ETHICAL DILEMMAS

Swiss financial services giant Credit Suisse recently announced that it missed red flags that could have alerted it to the alleged fraud perpetrated by its former -- and now bankrupt -- investment partner, Greensill Capital. Those missed signals cost Credit Suisse $10 billion in investor funds it can't regain, as well as $43 million in pay from the 10 people it fired, along with a restructuring of its entire asset management arm.

Credit Suisse is not alone. Many other businesses around the world and throughout Germany are dealing with the same financial fallout – all because, according to Credit Suisse, a tiny handful of managers and employees failed to "behave appropriately."

This probably comes as no surprise to the one in five German employees (22%) who say they have personally seen or have firsthand knowledge of unethical workplace behavior, according to Gallup research conducted in late 2021.

What may surprise their leaders is that the majority of those employees (63%) say they did not report the inappropriate behavior they witnessed. Gallup data indicate it's primarily because those employees didn't trust their company to do the right thing or weren't sure what the right thing was. In any case, most of the German employees who saw red flags walked on by.

Those workers missed a chance to gain clarity and reassurance from their boss. They lost an opportunity to gain trust in – and from – their leaders. Some of them missed the moment to head off a crisis (Nink & Robison, 2022).

Destructive leadership is most prevalent when power and influence are transactional and communication travels in a top-down manner creating asymmetrical forms of communication with unguarded messages down the chain of command. It takes decentralized decision-making, adaptive culture, and a trustworthy, accountable style of leadership to keep destructive leaders in check. Followers and stakeholders throughout the organization need to have the strength and moral courage to speak up and hold these leaders accountable and focus on changing their behaviors during the good times, so that during disruptive times, the temptation to use destructive behaviors will be diminished (Belasen, 2016).

Upward Mobility

Yet another aspect of this invincibility is the fact that senior executives are saddled with a few qualifications required to rise to the top of the pyramid based on merit or performance. Often, they are recruited from outside after receiving a large severance package (the "golden parachute") while their old company is undergoing major transition (e.g., restructuring, mergers and acquisitions) enabling senior executives to "land softly" in a new executive role at another company.

Evaluation of executive level skills is typically based on a combination of factors including a strong track record of exceeding performance expectations in senior roles, strategic thinking and the ability to influence important decisions, experience across business lines, driving significant bottom line results, and a well-connected network within and outside the organization.

A promotion to senior executive level from within is a more systematic process by which qualified middle managers are identified as successors, are nurtured through the leadership development pipeline, and elevated to senior leadership positions. Often, however, the credentials of middle managers are overlooked as they are passed over for promotion to senior executive levels because the rise from the ranks typically requires a different skillset, including a broader strategic vision, greater political acumen, and the ability to navigate high-level issues, which may not be as heavily developed in a middle management scope of responsibilities (Belasen & Belasen, 2016).

WHY YOU DIDN'T GET THAT PROMOTION

Executive placement decisions hinge on three categories of skills: *nonnegotiable*, without which you will not be considered for a promotion; *deselection factors*, which eliminate you as a candidate even if you're otherwise qualified; and *core selection factors*, which ultimately determine who gets the position. Leadership competency models typically fail to make these distinctions, and most don't spell out how skills should be demonstrated at different levels. In middle management, for instance, teamwork is a vital competency. At more senior levels, the imperatives are to think strategically and to acquire and develop talent. Many unwritten rules are especially elusive because they don't pertain to technical or business knowledge. Rather, they relate to the soft skills that give decision makers an intuitive sense of your potential for success. Complicating matters further, managers and HR professionals often give intentionally vague feedback, not direct constructive criticism – for fear of losing good employees. You'll need to dig deep to get useful input from executives and other colleagues: Project a sincere desire to understand what's holding you back. Ask questions, but don't lobby or argue. Avoid comments or gestures that convey defensiveness, which could cause the other person to clam up or move the conversation to safer territory. And be alert to code words and phrases – such as general observations about the need for "increased leadership ability" or "better communication" – that may mask fundamental issues (Beeson, 2009).

Arrogance

Corporate executives with special contributions to their organizations are likely to get away with a lack of accountability due to perceptions of being indispensable. This feeling of entitlement or self-righteousness allows them to get away with arrogant behavior or ignore criticisms associated with mistrust without regard to humility. These executives are aggressive, self-aggrandized, and driven to get results using unrestrained control of organizational resources, and the ability to manipulate outcomes, further eliciting unethical behavior (Chandler, 2009).

According to Finkelstein (2003), the leadership mindsets that keep top executives from correcting their courses of action include: dominant personality; having no boundaries between personal and corporate interests; having all the answers; disregarding colleagues who do not support their views; obsession with visibility and public image; rationalizing major obstacles in their strategy; and worshipping the status quo.

MITIGATING EXECUTIVE HUBRIS

The excessive pride and arrogance of some executives can create blind spots, leading them to ignore valuable feedback from others, make poor decisions and, in the worst cases, harm the well-being of others. Therefore, it is crucial for boards to identify and mitigate executive hubris to help protect the company's reputation and ensure its long-term success. Here are three ways boards can do this:

1. Identify excess narcissism

...Destructive narcissists prioritize personal power and use it to reinforce their exaggerated self-image, suppress any form of feedback and pursue ideas and projects that are grandiose in nature. It is important for a board to keep an eye out for these behaviors and look for subtle clues via language, mindset, behaviors and written or non-written communication to establish whether leadership behaviors are… congruent with balanced and stable leadership

2. Foster a culture of constructive feedback

Boards must ensure that the executives in charge of the organization are receptive to feedback and willing to listen to dissenting opinions. Leaders who are open to feedback are more likely to recognize their mistakes and take corrective action, helping prevent disastrous consequences for the company... Boards can encourage a culture of constructive feedback by regularly soliciting feedback from employees and stakeholders, using anonymous surveys or events using external consultants. Additionally, boards can ensure there are regular performance reviews that include feedback from peers, subordinates and external stakeholders to ensure executives receive regular and diverse feedback.

3. Encourage diversity at the board and C-suite levels

Boards can encourage and drive diversity by establishing diversity goals and **holding executives accountable** for meeting those goals. They can also create opportunities for diverse candidates to be considered for executive positions and enforce diversity as a strategic priority for the business (Reed, 2023).

Shift in Focus

Organizational leaders, executives, and managers, who fall short of balancing the leadership behaviors needed for leading complex organizational environments tend to think in terms of "either-or" dichotomies. They attach mutually exclusive categories (e.g., ingroup, outgroup) to people and values, form attitudes toward "desired" and "undesired" behaviors, and develop biases that align with their preferences. These biases are translated into mindsets, values, and patterned behaviors that guide their thinking and actions, often without regard to unintended consequences.

With cut-throat competition and pressure to demonstrate bottom line results, these corporate leaders fall prey to a *Success Syndrome* manifest in comparative ranking, monetary rewards, social status and prestige, and become blind to the values of trustworthiness and accountability. Success may cause leaders to excuse themselves from established protocols (Cameron, 2003), while making exceptions for their own behavior (Price, 2006). This sense of entitlement and rationalization, whereby leaders gratuitously expect certain rewards for their hard work triggers denial and further leads to a lack of accountability.

Moral awareness is a powerful medium which allows leaders to understand their strengths and weaknesses, what motivates them, and how they make decisions. Moral awareness and self-regulation are the starting points in a learning process aimed at identifying gaps between actual and desired behaviors and a tracking plan aimed at remedying deficiencies based on input from others. It helps move leaders from moral awareness to moral judgment (deciding which course of action is justifiable), to moral motivation (or the commitment to pursue actions), and moral character (or the persistence to sustain the behavior).

Trustworthy leaders can create a culture of accountability by making sure that managers and employees engage in transparent and ethical business practices. Establishing open communication channels and promoting high involvement, openly debating issues, sharing information and decision-making criteria and ensuring that policies and procedures are applied fairly and equitably, are vital means for boosting accountability.

Leaders who consistently share information about themselves and the organization and tie ethics to long-term success of the organization build a culture of trust with followers and enhance organizational credibility with stakeholders. When people are entrusted with all the necessary information to make wise choices, they are likely to act accountably and be recognized as trustworthy (Belasen & Eisenberg, 2023).

SMART Managers

Goal setting is a path that aligns individual, team, and organizational objectives by keeping team members motivated and by fostering a culture of accountability where constructive criticisms are welcome, and mistakes are seen as learning opportunities to hone new skills. This culture gives rise to honest dialogues, sharing updates and concerns, and soliciting feedback without fear.

This culture enables employees to stay focused and collaborate through teamwork and mutual trust. Team members understand the power of synergistic roles and skills while recognizing their joint accountability for achieving the overall goal. They feel comfortable sharing ideas, relying on each other's strengths, openly communicating, supporting one another, and working toward achieving a common goal.

To increase accountability through teamwork, middle managers set SMART objectives that are aligned with the company's strategic objectives, resulting in improved overall organizational performance. SMART objectives act as a motivational strategy that helps synchronize members' activities, holds them accountable for actions and results, and improves the collective performance of the team. These are:

1. **Specific**: Identifying the outcomes that team members are expected to achieve
2. **Measurable**: Outlining the milestones and metrics for measuring progress
3. **Achievable**: Ensuring that the proposed project or plan is realistic and that team members have the skills and resources to achieve their goals
4. **Relevant**: Confirming that the stated goals are beneficial for both professional development and the overall performance in the workplace
5. **Timely**: Setting a clear timeline with a starting and ending date

SMART managers also follow the principle of sufficiency. They provide structure and control, track progress, identify potential issues early on and adjust performance indicators for relevance and feasibility. Once members demonstrate high levels of commitment and competence toward achieving their stated goals, these managers shift their style from a direct approach to a more participative approach. They encourage cooperation and involvement of all team members, facilitate interactions, and empower team members to make decisions and take ownership of their work, fostering a sense of personal accountability.

This is the essence of situational leadership. Effective middle managers adapt their leadership style to fit the specific needs of the project following the team's stages of development and maturity level, replacing the single-minded, "one-size-fits-all" approach with flexibility, empowerment, and openness to new experiences. Empowering team members fosters transparency, encourages constructive feedback, and establishes a culture where team members have a sense of joint accountability.

Teamwork

Teamwork builds trust and promotes collaboration within the team, holding each other accountable for meeting deadlines and quality standards. To sustain employee accountability through teamwork, middle managers focus on establishing clear expectations, fostering open communication, encouraging mutual respect, providing regular feedback, and publicly acknowledging and celebrating individual contributions to team goals to motivate and reinforce positive behaviors. They stay ahead of the curve by showing willingness to learn new methods and demonstrate accountability by taking ownership of their own actions and failures, becoming positive role models for team members.

The inspiration to collaborate draws on strong ethics, teamwork, and cross-functional collaboration by promoting transparency, honesty, and accountability. Information is shared freely and rapidly, without filters or censors, to help foster innovation (Belasen & Luber, 2017). Team members have diverse backgrounds and use teamwork to jointly figure out solutions to problems. The collaborative workplace is supportive and dynamic with leaders serving as mentors and coaches. Individual development, high cohesion, morale, teamwork, and consensus are valued. Success is defined in terms of trust, mutual respect, and engagement. Individuals and teams are recognized and praised for initiating innovation and enhancing the quality of products and services that reach consumers.

Teamwork expands the traditional roles of middle managers into shared responsibility, mutual trust, and enhanced communication. It can take place within work units where members coach and mentor each other professionally and with mutual respect. Teamwork may also involve cross-functional teams where members of different departments cooperate and coordinate with one another to provide the best service to customers.

Table 5.1 outlines important criteria of team leadership behaviors and skills across eight dimensions: Team

Table 5.1 Behavioral Indicators

Dimension	*Boundaries*	*Priorities*	*Focus*	*Success factors*	*Competencies*
Team development	Team leader establishes open channels of communication; The leader creates a climate where people can share ideas and feelings and begin to identify and align with common objectives	Identify team structure and team dynamics	Common goals; Shared team responsibility	Obtaining external resources; Shaping brand identity and image; Enhancing reputation	Persuasion, effective presentation; Negotiating skills
Team leadership		Prioritize situational leadership approaches to managing team performance	Innovation flexibility	Identifying important trends; Facilitating change	Creative thinking; Intuition; Innovation skills

(Continued)

Table 5.1 (Continued) Behavioral Indicators

Dimension	*Boundaries*	*Priorities*	*Focus*	*Success factors*	*Competencies*
Promoting cooperation	Team leader emphasizes common purpose and establishes acceptable norms. The leader clarifies the process of communication and encourages dialogue and involvement	Clarify the goals for team members and the roles needed to accomplish these goals	Mentoring, coaching	Developing members' capacity; Inspiring action; Empathizing	Self-understanding; Active listening; Sensitivity skills
Facilitating meetings		Facilitate meetings and encourage participation in team activities	Engagement openness	Building cohesion and teamwork	Facilitation; problem-solving communication

(Continued)

Table 5.1 (Continued) Behavioral Indicators

Dimension	*Boundaries*	*Priorities*	*Focus*	*Success factors*	*Competencies*
Resolving conflict	Team leader encourages interdependence and reduces tensions and conflicts;	Recognize sources of conflict and means to resolve them	Stability control	Maintaining the structure and flow of information; promoting consistency	Scheduling, organizing, coordinating; managing crises
Acting ethically	Promotes ownership and commitment; integrity and transparency	Distinguish ethical from unethical group decisions and behaviors	Integrity quality Improvement	Tracking non-compliance; evaluating facts and details	Handling data and forms; reviewing behaviors and outcomes

(Continued)

Table 5.1 (Continued) Behavioral Indicators

Dimension	*Boundaries*	*Priorities*	*Focus*	*Success factors*	*Competencies*
Meeting team goals	Team members are committed to team shared goals and have a clear understanding of expectations and responsibilities; team leader provides guidance for continuous improvement; team members are given opportunities to assume leadership	Recognize the importance of synergy and integrative solutions	Direction goal clarity	Clarifying expectations; defining roles and responsibilities	Critical thinking; execution
Sustaining excellence		Support the team goals and the need for joint accountability	Outcome evaluation	Motivating to accept joint accountability	Managing time and stress; working productively

Source: Belasen, A. (2022). *Resilience in Healthcare Leadership: Practical Strategies and Self-Assessment Tools*, New York, NY, Routledge.

Table 5.2 Teamwork Survey

Instructions: *Rate how strongly you agree or disagree with each of the following statements by placing your responses twice: One for current, the other for desired.* **Level of Agreement** *1 – Strongly disagree* *2 – Disagree* *3 – Neither agree nor disagree* *4 – Agree* *5 – Strongly agree*			
		Current	**Desired**
	I am knowledgeable about the dynamics of team development		
	I help team members establish trusting relationships		
	I help the team work more efficiently and productively		
Team Development AVERAGE			
	I initiate action to accomplish team goals		
	I have a good sense of the team's trajectory		
	I understand the value of synergy in inspiring team members		
Team Leadership AVERAGE			
	I inspire group members to achieve common goals		
	I help clarify roles and shared responsibilities		
	I promote cooperation through trust and mutual respect		

(*Continued*)

Table 5.2 (Continued) Teamwork Survey

Promoting Cooperation AVERAGE			
	I develop the agenda in consultation with team members		
	I provide information and relevant material		
	I encourage participation and contributions from others		
Facilitating Meetings AVGERAGE			
	I suggest ways that integrate different viewpoints		
	I use active listening during disagreements		
	I offer ideas to reach consensus		
Resolving Conflict AVGERAGE			
	I place my concern for the group ahead of my own		
	I am respectful and sensitive to the other members		
	I treat members equally and equitably		
Acting Ethically AVERAGE			
	I value group decision making		
	I collaborate with others		
	I support the outcomes of group decision making		

(*Continued*)

Table 5.2 (Continued) Teamwork Survey

Meeting Goals AVERAGE			
	I create opportunities for new development		
	I recognize and reward excellent performance		
	I pursue long term goals for my team		
Sustaining Excellence AVERAGE			

development, team leadership, promoting cooperation, facilitating meetings, resolving conflict, acting ethically, meeting team goals, and sustaining excellence. Since team dynamics are based on shared-responsibilities, team members take turns leading the team's direction. The survey in Table 5.2 is designed to measure the effectiveness of teamwork considering these eight dimensions.

Team leadership evolves through phases with each characterized by different needs and goals. For example, transitioning from a functional group to a highly interdependent team requires a team charter with goals and objectives, positive attitudes and team norms, clear tasks and metrics, performance strategy, effective communication, trust, and feedback. Moving toward action requires analytics, tracking systems, coordination, engagement and maintenance of positive relationships and well-synchronized effort. To accomplish this, a driving force must be present – a trustworthy and accountable leader.

Figure 5.1 shows the ratings across the eight dimensions of teamwork. The scores are calculated by averaging the ratings across the dimensions. The differences between the current and desired ratings are denoted in percentage points for each

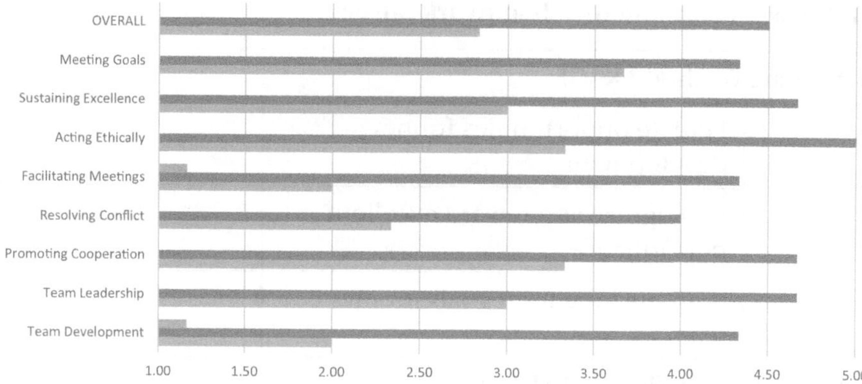

	Team Development	Team Leadership	Promoting Cooperation	Resolving Conflict	Facilitating Meetings	Acting Ethically	Sustaining Excellence	Meeting Goals	OVERALL
%chg	116.67%	55.56%	40.00%	71.43%	116.67%	50.00%	55.56%	18.18%	58.82%
Desired	4.33	4.67	4.67	4.00	4.33	5.00	4.67	4.33	4.50
Current	2.00	3.00	3.33	2.33	2.00	3.33	3.00	3.67	2.83

Figure 5.1 Dimensions of Teamwork

dimension, helpful for rank ordering the dimensions, and prioritizing improvement efforts.

The assessment method helps to visually detect the differences across the eight dimensions, solicit thoughts and ideas about causes and interventions, prioritize areas for improvement, and agree on time to review results. It also helps to support the team's effort to develop a meaningful conversation about problems and brainstorm ideas for further improvement. For example, both "team development" and "facilitating meetings" reflect much larger gaps and could be ranked higher on the priority list of team members. Interventions may include team building, goal setting, time management, coaching, and mentoring.

Retaking the survey periodically and plotting the results on new diagrams can help the team to review its progress over time. Middle managers and team leaders can use similar charts to map the responses of members over time, with follow-ups to discuss the results, explore the team's learning experience and underscore the options for continuous improvement.

Accountability Through High Reliability

Accountability is a core principle of high-reliability organizations (HROs), which are organizations that consistently operate safely and effectively in high-risk environments. HROs use accountability to improve performance and create a culture of safety where employees at every level take responsibility for identifying and reporting potential risks, errors, or near misses. With a strong emphasis on transparency and open communication, everyone in the HRO is held accountable for high standards and for preventable errors. According to Weick and Sutcliffe (2007), HRO principles include:

Sensitivity to operations: Preserving situational awareness by senior executives, middle managers, of systems and work processes that affect the delivery of quality outcomes. Having awareness is key to noting risks, closing loopholes in processes where there is potential for preventable errors.

Reluctance to simplify: Avoiding overly simple explanations of failure (e.g., unqualified staff, inadequate training, and communication failure) is essential to underscore the reasons for risks and preventable errors. Ask "why" and "what if" questions, solicit expert advice, swap the dominant explanation with diverse perspectives from others. Leverage new thinking to get to root causes problems.

Preoccupation with failure: Examine near misses to avoid repeated occurrences and learn from experience to improve quality. Identifying and fixing problems is everyone's responsibility and is supported by leadership.

Deference to expertise: Senior executives and middle managers are open to insights and suggestions by employees and specialists at customer interface points about potential risks and preventable errors.

Resilience: Leaders and staff need to be well prepared to handle quickly and effectively with system failures.

Middle managers actively promote a culture of safety and continuous improvement, ensure that information flows seamlessly up-and-down the chain, and empower staff to speak up about potential issues without fear of retribution. They model accountability by demonstrating a commitment to safety practices, encouraging employees to report near misses and potential hazards, and ensuring that those concerns are addressed promptly and effectively. Middle managers use open communication channels and engage routinely with customer interface employees to gather feedback on workflow processes, identify potential risks, and implement necessary changes based on their insights.

Middle managers also delegate decision-making authority to staff members to make timely decisions within their scope of responsibility, allowing them to take ownership of work outcomes, and contribute to problem-solving. They examine incidents thoroughly to understand underlying causes, implement preventive measures, and improve by learning from failures.

Middle managers lead accountability efforts by anticipation and prediction rather than reaction. They meet in daily operational briefs where they look back to learn from failures and look forward to lessening failures. They conduct frequent walk-rounds to reinforce consistent behaviors, find, and fix critical implementation issues, and recognize and reward employees who proactively contribute to safety and quality improvement initiatives.

Overall, middle managers are crucial to the success of an HRO by actively promoting a culture of safety, ensuring open communication, and empowering employees to contribute to continuous improvement at the operational level. They are responsible for translating the HRO principles into actionable practices at the operational level by acting as a bridge between senior leadership and frontline employees.

Conclusion

Accountability is crucial for driving performance, maintaining alignment, and promoting a culture of ownership within the workplace. When individuals and teams are accountable, operational goals are aligned with broader organizational strategies, potential gaps are addressed early on, and proactive measures can be taken to mitigate risks.

Middle managers play a key role in shaping a culture of accountability by modeling ethical behavior, upholding standards, and consistently reinforcing the importance of responsibility. They use their location within the hierarchy to cascade organizational goals and priorities down to frontline teams, bridging potential gaps between upper management and frontline employees. This ensures that everyone understands their role and the significance of achieving strategic goals.

These high-level, strategic goals act as the guiding framework for setting SMART, actionable day-to-day operational objectives, and holding teams responsible for achieving these objectives. Middle managers encourage personal and joint accountability through teamwork by promoting empowerment and ownership, and by actively monitoring individual and team performance. They provide coaching and development using open communication channels, and help employees improve their performance and develop accountability skills.

A culture of accountability can boost employee morale and engagement by providing clarity and a sense of purpose, by driving productivity and improving overall results. This creates a strong dynamic where trust empowers middle managers to delegate tasks and provide autonomy, while accountability ensures that employees are held responsible for their actions, ultimately leading to win–win outcomes, enhancing satisfaction and engagement and driving organizational success.

References

Beeson, J. (2009). Why you didn't get that promotion, June, *HBR.* https://hbr.org/2009/06/why-you-didnt-get-that-promotion.

Belasen, A. (2016). Deception and failure: Mitigating leader-centric behaviors. In A. Belasen & R. Toma (Eds.), *Confronting Corruption in Business: Trusted Leadership, Civic Engagement* (pp. 183–216), New York, Routledge.

Belasen, A. & Luber, E. (2017). Innovation implementation: Leading from the middle out. In Nicole Pfeffermann & Julie Gould, (Eds.). Strategy and Communication for Innovation: Integrative Perspectives on Innovation in the Digital Economy, pp. 229-243, Germany: Springer.

Belasen, A. (2022). *Resilience in Healthcare Leadership: Practical Strategies and Self-Assessment Tools.* New York, NY, Routledge.

Belasen, A. T. & Belasen, A. R. (2016). Value in the middle: Cultivating middle managers in healthcare organizations. *Journal of Management Development*, 35(9), 1149–1162.

Belasen, A. T. & Eisenberg, B. (2023). Building trust for better crisis communication: Lessons for leadership development. Chapter 7 in Nicole Pfeffermann & Monika Schaller (Eds.), *New Leadership Communication - Inspire Your Horizon* (pp. 93–110), Switzerland, Springer. https://doi.org/10.1007/978-3-031-34314-8_7.

Bentega.io. (2024). Metrics and performance accountability, October 29. https://www.bentega.io/blog/metrics-and-performance-accountability.

Cameron, K. (2003). Ethics, virtuousness, and constant change. In N. M. Tichy & A. R. McGill (Eds.), *The Ethical Challenge: How to Lead with Unyielding Integrity* (pp. 85–94), San Francisco, CA, Jossey-Bass.

Chandler, D. J. (2009). The perfect storm of leaders' unethical behavior: A conceptual framework. *International Journal of Leadership Studies*, 5(1), 69–93.

Covey, S.M.R. (2008). *The Speed of Trust.* Simon & Schuster.

Finkelstein, M. (2003). *Why Smart Executives Fail.* New York, NY: Penguin Books.

Garrido-Moreno, A., Martín-Rojas, R., & García-Morales, V. J. (2024). The key role of innovation and organizational resilience in improving business performance: A mixed-methods approach. *International Journal of Information Management*, 7, https://www.sciencedirect.com/science/article/pii/S0268401224000252.

Herne, K., Lappalainen, O., Setälä, M. *et al.* (2022). Accountability as a warrant for trust: An experiment on sanctions and justifications in a trust game. *Theory Decision,* 93, 615–48. https://doi.org/10.1007/s11238-021-09864-7.

Kemp, A. (2024). Most unethical behavior goes unreported and unresolved. *Gallup*, September 24. https://www.gallup.com/workplace/648770/unethical-behavior-goes-unreported-unresolved.aspx.

Nink, M. & Robison, J. (2022). Ethical dilemmas: What to do when employees stay silent. *Gallup*, May 3. https://www.gallup.com/workplace/392207/ethical-dilemmas-employees-stay-silent.aspx.

Price, T. L. (2006). *Understanding Ethical Failures in Leadership.* New York, NY: Cambridge University Press.

Reed, A. (2023). Three ways a board can help identify and mitigate executive hubris. *Forbes*, April 18. https://www.forbes.com/councils/forbescoachescouncil/2023/04/18/three-ways-a-board-can-help-identify-and-mitigate-executive-hubris/.

Sheedy, E. & Canestrari-Soh, D. S. B. (2023). Does executive accountability enhance risk management and risk culture? *Accounting and Finance,* 63(4), 4093–4124.

Weick, K. E. & Sutcliffe, K. M. (2007). *Managing the Unexpected: Resilient Performance in the Age of Uncertainty* (2nd ed.). Jossey-Bass.

Chapter 6

Demonstrating Credibility

 DOI: 10.4324/9781003608028-6

Introduction

Credibility and character are perceptions held by others of a person's combination of trustworthiness, expertise, dependability, and empathy. Under different conditions, one or more of those traits may emerge as most important. However, for leaders tackling disruptions, if any one of the four traits is removed, credibility is likely to suffer. Leaders gain credibility when they project compassion and demonstrate that they understand the risks and probable impact of decisions and actions. They are aware of their weaknesses and have the humility to defer to experts and delegate responsibilities to middle managers.

Lack of credibility may lead to employee distrust and disengagement, adversely affecting the perceptions of the competence and trustworthiness of leaders as well as the overall reputation of the organization. However, when leaders are engaged in transparent, honest, accountable, and credible behaviors they also give more attention to self-reflection which can result in improving the perceptions of their trustworthiness and credibility (Belasen & Belasen, 2025). Leaders who share information about themselves and the organization, and who tie ethics and diversity to the long-term success of the organization build a culture of trust with followers and enhance their personal credibility with stakeholders.

We begin this chapter by describing the meaning and significance of having personal and organizational credibility along with the risks associated with lack of credibility. We then discuss the merits of maintaining high levels of credibility both internally and externally. Finally, we use assessment instruments to chart the dimensions of credibility and how middle managers can use these assessments to improve their performance.

Credibility as a Dimension of Trust

Credibility is a strength that aligns words with deeds. It is demonstrated by the level of consistency between leaders' values, beliefs, principles, and ideals and their behaviors and practices. Credibility is essential for establishing a positive rapport between leaders and followers. Employees are more likely to bond with their organization, experience a strong sense of identity in aligning their beliefs with the mission of the organization, and commit to organizational goals when they perceive their immediate managers as credible (Kouzes & Posner, 2012).

A gap in credibility reflects a disconnect between what leaders say and what they do. Inconsistent behaviors or broken promises tend to reduce the perceived credibility of leaders. When left unaddressed, a lack of credibility may trigger mistrust and cynicism by employees, affect their morale and the motivation to engage, and lead to loss of productivity (Williams et al., 2022).

Communicating consistently about decisions and ensuring that disseminated information is not contradictory, making sure that promises are kept, and that employees are not confused or left in the dark are the cornerstones for building trust and credibility. It means actively leading by example, following through on promises, demonstrating competence and reliability through consistent actions and communication, being authentically honest, having emotional intelligence, and acting in line with the stated values.

Trust is built on credibility and is preserved through social interactions. It is also important for leaders to be accountable for their contributions, even when they lead to poor results, show respect and provide constant support to employees. At times of disruption when trust is fragile, it is important to initiate deliberate efforts to mitigate distrust, clarify goals and messaging strategies, and demonstrate unwavering commitment to ethical principles.

As mentioning in Chapter 4, cohesive messaging by the Singaporean government, with an understanding that detailed knowledge matters and that the health and economic risks were asymmetrically distributed helped build trust and credibility in their communication. The communication was consistently clear and evidence based, enhancing leadership credibility, and boosting public trust.

In many organizations, the COVID-19 pandemic, which triggered social isolation due to lockdown restrictions and the increase in quarantine measures, also disrupted the trusting relationships between employees and managers. Replacing site-based workplaces with virtual or hybrid formats with limited in-person communication has shattered trust in many remote work settings. Research conducted during COVID-19 shows that managers are struggling with the effective management of remote employees, ultimately eroding employees' trust in the managers' credibility to accurately assess their performance (Parker et al., 2020).

Van Zoonen et al. (2024) examined the mediating role of communication frequency and quality in the relationship between workplace isolation and trust. Their findings show that the negative relationship between isolation and trust was caused primarily by limited face-to-face communication and poor quality of shared information with profound impact on manager–employee relationships.

Employees who work remotely are less visible, miss opportunities for recognition or career advancement, and feel a potential supervisory bias against them compared to their office-based colleagues. Fearing the stigma of being "out of sight, out of mind" due to reduced visibility and limited opportunities for interaction, they begin to lose trust in their managers, further fueling misinterpretations, difficulty gauging genuine feedback, and the perception of being overly monitored and micromanaged. These feelings further magnify stress levels and increase turnover intentions. Abusive supervision through sustained display of hostile verbal and non-verbal behaviors, when unmitigated, can encourage peers to engage in similar unethical behaviors, leading to affected employees feeling emotionally drained and insecure (Li et al., 2022).

It is, therefore, important for managers to build and sustain personal and professional relationships with employees and teams. While achieving organizational goals and deadlines can contribute to collaborative and motivating work environments, leaders must also be attentive to the needs of their teams. When leaders show empathy and apply active listening in their communications, they also create powerful incentives for aligning employees with the prevailing values and beliefs on which trust is built, and credibility thrives.

Senior executives and middle managers can provide support by hosting employee recognition ceremonies, encouraging mentorship, initiating training and professional development, and creating succession planning programs. Leaders who demonstrate empathy in the workplace improve their credibility and increase trust and collaboration. Employees who feel valued and supported by their leaders are motivated to perform with added energy and renewed commitment. When employees' beliefs align with their company's mission and values, they tend to be more engaged and motivated in their work, find deeper meaning and purpose in their contributions, and are more accomplished, productive, and loyal to the organization.

Building Credibility

Lipman (2018) describes five time-tested ways to foster credibility. While there are certainly many more (as Lipman admits) these five are particularly crucial and effective.

Leaders who are trustworthy and credible deliver results: Credibility is directly related to results. Everyone loves a winner, right?

Transparency: The feeling of a need to sugar-coat, cushion, or hide things from subordinates is an outdated notion and one that decreases credibility. Withholding relevant information from employees creates the appearance of dishonesty and leads to resentment. Be clear and thoughtful when communicating and there will be less ripples in the communication stream.

Don't duck tough decisions: This is why managers are given important responsibilities and the power to make decisions. Managers are trusted to contemplate big, difficult, organizational choices.

Consistent behavior: People love consistency and routine. They respond positively when their leaders act in a predictable manner and poorly when their leaders' words and deeds are misaligned.

Lead by example: There is nothing worse than a manager who plays by their own set of rules. Employees watch their managers closely, so why not set a good example in following ethical standards? Saying one thing and doing another will rapidly diminish credibility.

So, why is it so important for senior executives and middle managers to be credible? Organizational leaders are the "face" of the company. They shape the perception of the company's identity, both externally and internally. Externally, they shape the company's image. Internally, they shape nearly every aspect of employees' behavior. Employees are unlikely to have positive attitudes in the workplace if they perceive their managers as lacking trust and credibility. Thoughts such as, "I could have done it better" will creep into an employee's mindset if they don't see their manager demonstrating competence. An employee with this mindset is unlikely to be productive, positive, or work collaboratively, resulting in lower morale and productivity.

If a leader cannot be trusted, an employee is likely to think that it is not important for them to act in a trustworthy way. Employees will emulate the actions of their leaders, both good and bad. Leaders should model the way by demonstrating trustworthiness with trickle down effects as employees who view their leader as trustworthy are likely to view the organization more positively as a whole. This leads to higher levels of employee engagement, satisfaction, and retention as well as to the perception of the organization as a trusted company.

BOOSTING CUSTOMER TRUST

Every business leader knows that trust is critical to a company's success and that lost trust often has financial consequences. An Economist magazine analysis of Volkswagen, Wells Fargo, and six other corporations calculated that a company loses 30% of its value when it loses trust, at least in the short term.

Conversely, an increase in trust can have financial rewards. The most trustworthy companies have outperformed the S&P 500, and high-trust companies are more than 2.5 times more likely to be high-performing revenue organizations. Our own research shows that trusted companies outperform their peers by up to 400% in terms of total market value, that customers who trust a brand are 88% more likely to buy again, and that 79% of employees who trust their employer are more motivated to work and less likely to leave (Reichheld & Dunlop, 2022).

Credibility with Stakeholders

Brand image in business refers to customers' perceptions of a company's reliability in delivering quality products and services. Businesses build their brands by creating and projecting unique identity that differentiates them from competitors and that resonates with their target audience.

Trust plays a crucial role in driving purchases and influences customers' preferences. Service quality, safety and reliability, and price perception significantly affect the consumers' perceptions of trust and purchasing decisions. Consumers are much more likely to buy a product or service from a brand they trust, as it reduces perceived risk and increases confidence in the quality of the products.

Lack of credibility may affect customer loyalty and retention as customers are less likely to purchase products or services rendered by businesses they do not trust. This undoubtedly may result in a higher churn rate (i.e., the percentage of customers who quit the business) as well as affect the overall reputation of the organization.

> Indeed, when institutional investors were asked to rate the importance of various factors in their investment decisions, very few prioritized companies' ability to maintain low earnings volatility. More important to them were management teams' credibility and willingness to take risks with the long term in mind (McKinsey & Company, 2021).

Diminishing levels of trust may also trigger a credibility gap that may erode brand value. Leaders who embody ethical principles inspire confidence and loyalty among stakeholders while also enhancing organizational credibility and reputation. Leadership credibility, consistently delivering on promises and maintaining a trustworthy reputation, is crucial for long-term success and viability.

Credibility builds a positive brand image, fosters customer loyalty and repeat purchases, attracts new customers, and builds trust with stakeholders, ultimately leading to financial stability, a sustainable business model, and opportunities for future growth. A strong reputation that is built on credibility helps companies curb economic downturns or mitigate market disruptions better than those with a poor image impacting their profitability and market share.

TRUST: IT ACCELERATES THE BOTTOM LINE

Trust in many institutions is declining, which is why it's at a premium in business. In our fourth trust survey, the results underscore the importance and the opportunity of trust among business executives, consumers, and employees. Among respondents, 95% of business executives agree that organizations have a responsibility to build trust (up from 92% in 2023). The numbers for consumers and employees are nearly as high, at 92% and 94%, respectively (unchanged in the past year). There isn't just a moral case for building trust – there's a business case as well, with 93% of business executives agreeing that the ability to build and maintain trust improves the bottom line.

Our data highlights an opportunity for companies to build trust with key stakeholders. Given the importance of trust, companies that understand their trust levels among employees, consumers, investors, and other stakeholders – and take a proactive approach to building it – can give themselves a clear edge over competitors (PWC, 2024).

Furthermore, engaging stakeholders in the strategic planning process facilitates the synthesis of diverse perspectives and insights, enriching the strategic discourse and enhancing the adaptability of organizational strategies. By incorporating stakeholder feedback into decision-making processes, leaders can proactively identify emerging challenges, seize latent opportunities, and tailor strategies to align with evolving market dynamics and stakeholder expectations.

One of these challenges involves teleworking. Given the shift to hybrid workplaces, a major challenge for leaders is to facilitate effective and open channels of communication with virtual employees. The social skills involved in effective face-to-face communication may not be easily transferred to virtual environments. Leaders need to develop effective communication skills, select suitable communication tools, use cultural intelligence skills, provide positive feedback to their teams, and recognize individual and team performance.

Credibility in Teleworking

Hybrid and remote work appeal to many employees despite possible pitfalls like blurring the boundaries between work and life, social isolation, loss of visibility to management for promotional consideration, and data security concerns. On the other hand, managers who remain entrenched in a process-driven framework rather than a result-oriented work environment may find telework to be unpalatable, due to their inability to monitor work. If the attractiveness of remote work continues to increase, it follows that companies unwilling to offer full or hybrid remote work options may risk losing top talent and suffer potentially significant losses in productivity and turnover costs.

67% OF U.S. EMPLOYERS TO LOSE EMPLOYEES TO REMOTE WORK IN 2024

Amazon CEO Andy Jassy made a bombshell announcement mandating employees' fulltime return to office work by January 2025, and the tech giant's workforce isn't having any of it.

In a striking comeback, nearly 75% of Amazon employees have stated they are seriously considering looking for another job, due to Amazon's rigorous in-office work policy, per a Blind survey conducted the day after the announcement.

Meanwhile, "four out of five Amazon professionals polled by Blind said they knew someone at the company who was considering looking for another job because of the in-office work policy, and 32% said they knew someone who had already quit in response," the Blind poll report continued.

Amazon is not the only U.S. company to lose its workers over the RTO debate. In its analysis which led to the findings in the 2024 Global Workforce Report, Remote.com revealed that within the past six months alone, 67% of U.S. employers have lost their talent force to competitors offering more flexible work strategies such as remote and hybrid-remote work; while an estimated 73% of employers globally (in the 10 countries where the survey was conducted) have lost their employees for the same reason – failing to provide remote work options (Wells, 2024).

For telework to thrive, managers must shift their mindset and focus on flexibility, results, and trust. They must also spend some time carefully creating metrics and objectives by which employees will be evaluated, and cultivating a team culture which recognizes wins and prioritizes communication. Companies that encourage flexible management styles are better positioned to realize the potential of teleworking, rebuild trust, improve communication, and facilitate social interactions as the means for increasing employee motivation.

HYBRID WORK ARRANGEMENT

According to Gallup research, 76% of full-time hybrid workers in the United States most often cite improved work–life balance as a top advantage of hybrid work. This sentiment is even clearer among exclusively remote workers, with 85% saying that improved work–life balance is among the greatest benefits of remote work.

For many workers without flexible work arrangements, working from home at least some of the time has a strong appeal. A Gallup survey of 21,543 U.S. employees conducted May 11–25, 2024, found that a majority (61%) of on-site workers working a full-time job with remote capability would prefer a hybrid work arrangement and an additional 28% would prefer to be fully remote (Kemp, 2024).

Hybrid workplaces create challenges for middle managers including developing methods for sharing expectations and collaborating with teams to prioritize projects and tasks. They make themselves available for feedback and suggestions and treat team members as partners. Gallup and Workhuman (2024) outlined essential practices that enable organizations to put their people at the center of their success regardless of whether they are working in an on-site, hybrid or exclusively remote work environment. These practices are listed below.

Set realistic performance goals collaboratively by involving employees in conversations about setting reasonable performance targets that align with a healthy work–life balance.

Uplift employees and communicate values through recognition by publicly acknowledging their contributions. Recognition acts as a positive reinforcement, motivating individuals to repeat desired behaviors by acknowledging and valuing their efforts and accomplishments.

Elevate well-being for all employees by applying human-centric business practices to drive meaningful improvements in the employee experience across work locations. Middle managers shift to a transformational leadership style by promoting learning, experimentation, and adaptation.

As organizations navigate these dynamics, leaders must adapt their approaches to accommodate the evolving landscape of work, harness technology, and foster a culture of collaborative innovation. Embracing the paradoxes inherent in digital leadership environments and deploying diverse management styles allows middle managers to stay abreast of emerging technologies and best practices while fostering open innovation.

Remaining attentive to these changes is crucial for sustaining credibility as pressures toward building and sustaining adaptive cultures are mounting at an unprecedented pace. Middle managers can position their organizations at the forefront of digital transformation, playing a pivotal role by ensuring organizational readiness to meet the challenges of digital transformation.

Credibility Through Adaptive Leadership

Middle managers unwilling to change their mindset or accept the practices of a results-based work environment may resort to micromanaging, frequently monitoring employees, leading to erosion of their credibility as trustworthy leaders. Micromanagement breeds resentment and tarnishes the goodwill between managers and employees. If employees feel as though they are mistrusted, communication may break down, risk-taking and innovation may grind to a halt, inefficiency may increase, and productivity may plummet. Instead, middle managers need to be comfortable focusing on results and outcomes rather than processes, as employees will be invisible to them throughout the day, at least for large segments of time.

Adaptive leadership promotes exploration of new ideas, joint action through entrepreneurial engagement and high tolerance for risk taking behavior, learning, and innovation. Adaptive middle managers have the know-how and communication skills to facilitate and implement innovation as an important part of improving and changing organizational practices. They encourage forward thinking, drive creativity, model collaborative behavior, and reward breakthrough ideas.

Adaptive leaders are able to manifest transparency, accountability, credibility, and honesty in their behaviors – qualities that influence trustworthiness. Transparency enables trustworthy leaders to explore ideas more directly using open communication channels. Accountability reflects the importance of communicating and sharing relevant and timely information with employees and stakeholders. Credibility reinforces important goals and interests and the need to follow up on decisions, promises, and commitments. Honesty enables trustworthy leaders to promote equity, fairness, and moral courage while holding members to high standards of truthfulness.

Trustworthy managers acknowledge uncertainty, communicate with compassion, show understanding and are empathetic. They embrace paradoxical skills to identify integrative solutions to problems and use multiple means of communication to promote cooperation needed to achieve desired results. Messaging that appeals to the brand identity, history, and core values of the organization plays a key role in building credibility in trusting relationships, especially during major disruptions (Belasen & Belasen, 2019).

When communication is clear, empathetic, transparent, and frequent, internal dialogues are more positive and team members show more confidence in pursuing innovation and, at the same time, trust the ability of trustworthy leaders to avert unnecessary risks (Belasen & Eisenberg, 2023). During major changes, middle managers empower organizational members, promote mutual respect, emphasize moral ethics and integrity, use dialogue communication, embed empathy and authenticity in their leadership style, and model the way by asking the right questions.

Heifetz, Grashow, and Linsky (2009) outlined key success factors for adaptive leadership which focus on emotional intelligence, development, and character, fostering a culture of honesty, valuing diverse perspectives, and embracing change while empowering your team. These keys are listed below.

Get on the balcony. Take a broader perspective by moving back and forth between what needs to be done and the big picture. This high-level perspective helps middle managers spot trends and prevents them from unwittingly becoming a prisoner of the system. Ask yourself, what is changing? What inhibits change from happening? Who is going to be affected by the change? What are the chances for unintended consequences and how to mitigate their risks?

Identify the adaptive challenge. Routine challenges are made up of technical work that is clear, predictable, and consistent. Adaptive challenges require leveraging the synergistic effects of diverse people with complementary skills.

Regulate distress. Leaders must resolve the tension between having people feel the need to change and having them feel overwhelmed by the complexity of change. An adaptive leader must be attuned to collective distress and support adaptive work at a pace that meets the pain threshold of organizational members. Coach and guide people to accept new roles and responsibilities by clarifying goals and key values. Raise tough questions without exhibiting anxiety. Communicate with confidence and poise. Focus on building a strong foundation of credibility by being honest, transparent, and consistent in your words and actions, while also demonstrating competence and empathy.

Maintain disciplined attention. Build momentum by inspiring people to contribute and get involved in all aspects of managing change. As goals and processes become clearer over time, adaptive leaders will bring the focus back to operational effectiveness making sure that everyone is engaged in doing the right things right.

Give the work back to employees. Instill confidence in people. Encourage learning and innovative thinking, risk-taking and accountability. Empower people to jointly recognize problems and offer solutions that can be fine-tuned by teams to solve these problems.

Protect leadership voices from below. Avoid groupthink or conformity by fostering open communication, encouraging diverse perspectives, and creating a psychologically safe workplace where dissenting views are appreciated. People need a collective effort to understand, recognize and have their own problems and solutions. Diverse perspectives can provoke creative thinking. Play "Devil's Advocate" or designate someone to challenge prevailing assumptions, question the group's direction, and present alternative viewpoints. Encourage individual and shared accountability by ensuring that individuals and teams are responsible for their own ideas and behaviors.

THE EMERGING ROLES OF MIDDLE MANAGERS

It is in this organizational disequilibrium that middle managers are now stepping, finding their true niche, and adding their greatest value. They are now emerging as mid-level leaders, successfully spearheading change, precisely because of the skills that were honed when, as middle managers, their authority, and accountability were asymmetric. When a manager must accomplish something, with all the accountability but none of the authority over the resources to get the work done, the successful manager typically develops:

- Networking skills, helping to gain access to the widest range of possible resources

- Influencing skills, because if you can't compel someone to do the work, you must convince them that in doing the work, there is something in it for them
- Effective communication skills that clearly grab the attention of those above and below them
- Alignment skills, or the ability to get people from different places to see an issue in a similar way that resonates with what's important to them.

And, as it turns out, these talents and skills are precisely what are needed to manage and lead the kind of continuous change that organizations face every day (Gilbert, 2009).

Leading successfully in disruptive times requires behavioral flexibility, the ability to adjust actions, and strategies in response to changing circumstances, is crucial for success in disruptive environments. It enables middle managers to have the credibility to cope with new expectations, explore different approaches, and adapt to new opportunities in changing environments. At the same time, behavioral flexibility enables learning, professional growth, and the ability to see strengths in diversity and engage successfully with the world.

Assessing the Credibility of a Leader

Understanding self-perceptions of leaders' credibility helps prepare both current and future leaders to gain trust and communicate effectively. The assessment proposed in this chapter is based on the trustworthy leadership model described in this book in which the four dimensions – transparency, credibility, accountability, and honesty – must be present simultaneously to increase the propensity to act with trust.

The survey addresses the extent to which middle managers focus on traits and behaviors that enhance their credibility. The questions relate honesty in messaging, consistency, truthfulness, humility, welcoming feedback, and meeting others' expectations. The 18-item research instrument reflects the values associated with credibility (Belasen & Belasen, 2025) and consists of Likert-style response options with answers on a scale of 1 (I do not demonstrate this behavior) to 5 (I demonstrate this behavior to a great degree).

Respondents are asked to answer the questions twice, first as a manifestation of their "actual" behavior; and second, as a reflection of their "desired" behavior. Figure 6.1 transposes the two sets of responses to provide a single view of the gaps across the measures. Understandably, the ratings which denote actual behaviors, are lower than the ratings which represent desired behaviors. The gap between the two sets signifies opportunities for improvement.

To foster the alignment between actual behaviors and expectations from others, a self-assessment can be used periodically to determine how well a middle manager has evolved and honed trustworthy leadership that relates to credibility over time. Another option is to obtain feedback from relevant constituents (e.g., stakeholders, senior executives, board members) using the same survey to see what they think.

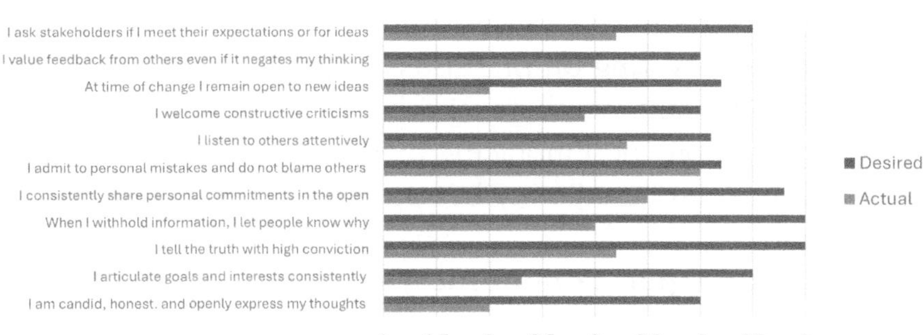

Figure 6.1 Assessment of Credibility

The differences between self-assessment and assessment from others could be very revealing and lead to a more valid and reliable understanding of how to bridge the gap. Ideas and actions for improvement or self-development could be prioritized to reflect inputs from others and eventually lead to a better alignment between the manager's views and the perceptions of credibility by others.

Leaders deficient in credibility may lose their reputation and the ability to marshal resources for the common good. Lack of credibility and trustworthiness lead to negative perceptions of the leader as being political and manipulative and who defers to authority rather than expertise to make solo decisions. These leaders tend to withhold information and resort to secrecy and closed-door decisions. By contrast, trustworthy and credible leaders lead by example and are transparent, accountable, and authentically honest. They are not only true to themselves but also help others to become more ethical and trusted individuals.

Conclusion

To increase a manager's credibility, key strategies include open communication and active listening to team members, providing meaningful feedback, demonstrating competence by making evidence-based decisions, communicating trust by consistently delivering on promises, delegating responsibilities, bonding with team members, and having personal interest in their development. Embracing these strategies should help establish trust and credibility between managers and team members:

Clear and Open Communication

- Communicate clearly and consistently with the team, underscoring key issues

- Practice active listening and use empathy to respond to concerns
- Be transparent about expectations, responsibilities, and decisions

Give and Receive Feedback

- Provide timely and relevant feedback to team members
- Be open to sharing ideas and suggestions with team members
- Use feedback to identify areas for improvement and leadership development

Demonstrate Personal Competence

- Be in the know about team's progress and need for resources
- Make evidence-based decisions
- Share relevant knowledge and expertise with the team

Communicate Trust

- Be consistent and follow through on commitments
- Recognize and celebrate team members' contributions
- Provide emotional support at times of disruption

Delegate and be Flexible

- Assign tasks and responsibilities based on individual competencies
- Provide resources and coaching to team members
- Encourage flexibility and participative decision-making within the team

Foster Relationships

- Get to know team members on a personal level
- Foster a positive work climate that is fair and inclusive
- Show strong interest in the professional and growth goals of team members

Model the Way

- Model the behaviors that team members are expected to emulate
- Demonstrate a strong work ethic by being responsible, punctual, and productive
- Be open to new experiences, admit mistakes, and learn from failure

Credibility, when demonstrated with strong honesty, transparency, and accountability, leads to building strong relationships and trust. Middle managers who incorporate active listening in their interpersonal communication, show genuine interest in others, treat everyone with respect and dignity, project self-assurance and competence while taking responsibility for mistakes, are also able to earn and maintain credibility.

References

Belasen, A. T. & Belasen, A. R. (2019). The strategic value of integrated corporate communication: Functions, social media, stakeholders. *International Journal of Strategic Communication*, 13, 4. https://doi.org/10.1080/1553118X.2019.1661842.

Belasen, A. T. & Belasen, A. R. (2025). Signaling trust during disruptions: Perceived gender differences in trustworthy leadership traits. *Gender in Management: An International Journal.* https://doi.org/10.1108/GM-04-2024-0187.

Belasen, A. T. & Eisenberg, B. (2023). Building trust for better crisis communication: Lessons for leadership development. Chapter 7 in Nicole Pfeffermann & Monika Schaller (Eds.), *New Leadership Communication – Inspire Your Horizon*, pp. 93–110, Switzerland, Springer. https://doi.org/10.1007/978-3-031-34314-8_7.

Gallup & Workhuman (2024). The human-centered workplace: Building organizational cultures that thrive. https://www.gallup.com/analytics/472658/workplace-recognition-research.aspx.

Gilbert, J. (2009). The sandwich generation: The emerging role of middle managers in organizational change. Paper presented at PMI® Global Congress 2009—North America, Orlando, FL. Newtown Square, PA: Project Management Institute.

Heifetz, R. A., Grashow, A., & Linsky, M. (2009). *The Practice of Adaptive Leadership: Tools and Tactics for Changing Your Organization and the World*. Boston, Mass.: Harvard Business Press.

Kemp, A. (2024). Employee wellbeing hinges on management, not work mode, *Gallup*, August 15, https://www.gallup.com/workplace/648500/employee-wellbeing-hinges-management-not-work-mode.aspx

Kouzes, J. M., & Posner, B. Z. (2012). *The Leadership Challenge: How to Make Extraordinary Things Happen in Organizations* (5th ed.). Chicago, Jossey-Bass.

Li, M., Ahmed, A., Syed, O. R., Khalid, N., & Muñoz, J. E., Jr (2022). Impact of abusive leader behavior on employee job insecurity: A mediating role of emotional exhaustion and abusive peer behavior. *Frontiers in Psychology*, 13, 947258. https://doi.org/10.3389/fpsyg.2022.947258.

Lipman, V. (2018). 5 time-tested ways to build leadership credibility. *Forbes,* March 27. https://www.forbes.com/sites/victorlipman/2018/03/24/5-time-tested-ways-to-build-leadership-credibility/?sh=75fdd76b3fa8.

McKinsey & Company. (2021). How executives can help sustain value creation for the long term, July 22. https://www.mckinsey.com/capabilities/strategy-and-corporate-finance/our-insights/how-executives-can-help-sustain-value-creation-for-the-long-term.

Parker, S. K., Knight, C., & Keller, A. C. (2020). Remote managers are having trust issues. *HBR*, July 30. https://hbr.org/2020/07/remote-managers-are-having-trust-issues.

PWC. (2024). Trust survey, March 12. https://www.pwc.com/us/en/library/trust-in-business-survey.html.

Reichheld, A. & Dunlop, A. (2022). 4 questions to measure — and boost — customer trust. November 1, *HBR*. https://hbr.org/2022/11/4-questions-to-measure-and-boost-customer-trust.

Van Zoonen, W., Sivunen, A. E., & Blomqvist, K. (2024). Out of sight – Out of trust? An analysis of the mediating role of communication frequency and quality in the relationship between workplace isolation and trust. *European Management Journal*, 42(4), 515–526

Wells, R. (2024). 67% Of U.S. employers to lose employees to remote work in 2024. *Forbes*, October 21. https://www.forbes.com/sites/rachelwells/2024/10/21/us-employers-to-lose-employees-to-remote-work-in-2024/.

Williams, R. I., Jr, Raffo, D. M., Randy Clark, W., & Clark, L. A. (2022). A systematic review of leader credibility: Its murky framework needs clarity. *Management Review Quarterly*, 1–44. Advance online publication. https://doi.org/10.1007/s11301-022-00285-6.

Chapter 7

Gaining Trust Through Honesty and Ethical Behavior

DOI: 10.4324/9781003608028-7

Introduction

Leading effectively in times of disruption requires the ability to build trust by providing psychological safety to followers through transparent communications, accountability for actions and results, credibility by esteeming followers to pursue their potential, and honesty rooted in unconditional kindness and reciprocity. Trusting relationships across hierarchical lines, especially between executives and middle managers, are developed when the parties feel confident in sharing their thoughts, feelings, and experiences without fear of judgment or retribution.

In the following sections, we explore key research findings and evidence from the field of leadership about the vital role that honesty plays in building trust with a focus on middle managers. An interesting extension is whether gender differences matter. Recent research involving middle managers suggests that on average women tend to be perceived as more honest than men in management roles, with studies often showing a correlation between female leadership and higher levels of ethical behavior, particularly when it comes to honesty and transparency (Belasen & Belasen, 2025). Earlier research linked gender to dishonesty and concluded that men are often more dishonest than women, particularly in competitive settings where lies advance self-interest (Kennedy & Kray, 2022).

Another important topic involves the significant impact that AI and analytical capabilities have on leadership roles. Automation and scalability through data-driven decision-making, more accurate insights into employee performance, and more reliable forecasts that inform strategic planning, allow senior executives to focus on higher level thinking and, at times, bypass middle managers.

A related topic is honesty as a strategic differentiator that sets an organization apart from competitors by building trust with customers and stakeholders, creating a positive reputation, and fostering loyalty and retention, especially in situations where other organizations might be less transparent or truthful. Hence, strong perceptions of honesty allow organizations to stand out by presenting themselves as more reliable and genuine in delivering products and services.

Another linkage in the context of international business is the tension that often arises between the leaders' own deeply held values and those of the host country's culture. Vogelgesang et al. (2009) illustrates how cultural intelligence moderates the relationship between authentic leadership and morally grounded cultural adaptation. Although it is important for leaders to possess cultural intelligence, they must also act authentically to avoid the pitfalls of merely imitating a host country's culture, which in the global context might lead to misunderstandings, unnecessary tensions, and missed opportunities to identify common grounds.

Bennis and Thomas (2002) argued that leadership evolves through transformative "crucibles," i.e., experiences that challenge leaders to rethink their identities and capabilities. Rooke and Torbert (2005) also explain that leaders undergo various transformations as they progress, with a key shift from an opportunistic to a strategic leader vital for middle managers who aspire to become senior executives. In the final analysis, modeling trustworthy leadership behavior rooted in honesty is key.

Why Honesty Is Important

Honesty is associated with altruistic behavior, positive social relations, truth telling, and reciprocal trust. Honesty may represent an important antecedent of trustworthiness impressions as even small signs of honesty lead people to reciprocate with more trust in subsequent interactions. Honesty breeds mutual respect and trusting relationships even when decisions are difficult to accept since building trust involves confidence in others' reliability, honesty, and competence.

A report by *Deloitte* (2019) *Global Human Capital Trends* showed that 80% of business and HR leaders worldwide believed they need to promote leadership capabilities with a focus on openness and honesty as precursors for building trust in organizations. A deficiency in honesty, however, may prove to be the most difficult to remedy, since it relies on the individual's self-awareness and the ability to open the communication channels and empathize with others, especially direct reports.

Trust in leadership is sustained through honesty, high personal integrity, and authenticity. When a top executive employs self-regulation and shows genuine concern for affected people or makes a personal sacrifice for others, a true form of trustworthy leadership emerges. Self-regulation is the ability to control personal behaviors, emotions, and thoughts achieve desired goals. Acting authentically, ensuring employees' safety, treating them with respect, and making sacrifices that benefit them, generates a high level of commitment to the leader and organizational goals.

Creating a culture of honesty and openness that celebrates ethical behavior and publicly acknowledging and rewarding individuals who uphold the highest levels of personal integrity and mindfulness through symbols and action promotes trust in and around organizations. Mindfulness allows leaders to reframe the situation by relying on divergent thinking and the ability to see events from multiple lenses.

RESEARCH HAS FOUND TRUST IN MIDDLE MANAGERS IS LOW, SO HOW DO WE IMPROVE THE SITUATION?

Recent corporate scandals have put the spotlight on the importance of business performance of customer trust. But trust between colleagues is just as important. Yet new research by CMI and leadership events specialist Top Banana has found that only one in three (36%) of the 1,456 UK managers surveyed for the *Middle Manager Lifeline* report "fully trust" their senior leaders. However, 72% of senior leaders believe that they're "highly trusted as managers.'"

Why should we care about this difference between perception and reality? Because middle managers are pivotal to organizational success. They are the connectors; the links between senior teams and those delivering operationally; the points of contact for customers, stakeholders, and divisions; the motivators keeping morale high when pressure rises. A breakdown in trust between middle managers and those at the top is bad news for productivity.

The Underlying Problem

Given that 85% of business leaders and managers agree trust is crucial to business performance, it's surprising that leaders don't take more opportunities to share feedback and business updates, and welcome greater input from their middle managers. Two in five (41%) middle managers said their organization's management style was bureaucratic, which can prevent the creativity and collaboration that helps many firms thrive.

Filtering information through the ranks is key to ensuring that middle managers feel invested in the business' future and performance. The saying goes that you're only as strong as your weakest link; without clear communication from the top middle managers are unable to do their job effectively and neither can their teams. The *Middle Manager Lifeline* survey revealed that only 31% of managers are "very confident" in communicating company strategy and guidance to their teams. Senior leaders should therefore invest more time in nurturing their teams and being more open. Middle managers want to understand senior management's thinking on important issues (63%) and see them be able to admit their mistakes (54%).

Bridging the Trust Gap

HR teams must help open communication between colleagues, providing management skills development and making sure middle managers are equipped to understand the language of senior management and relay it to their teams. The need for such development is clear: only 31% of managers feel "very confident" in their ability to communicate company strategy to their staff.

In addition, the *Middle Manager Lifeline* sets out a practical framework consisting of five essential elements to guide organizations in creating an open culture that will bridge the trust gap:

Communications – committing to an open and honest relationship with middle managers.
Integrity – challenging everyone, regardless of seniority, to act according to stated values.
Visibility – ensuring those at the top are seen to be accountable for their actions and open to challenge.
Interactions – creating meaningful opportunities for colleagues to meet and feed back to senior management.
Connections – investing in training and development at all levels to equip them with professional skills to communicate and manage their teams (Woodman, 2016).

Applying Woodman's (2016) framework can enable middle managers to become more agile, effective, and connected than ever before. Leaders can recognize and support middle managers, creating an open and honest environment, to enable them to thrive and act as key connectors across organizations.

Honesty and Fear

Honesty and fear often exist in a complex relationship, where fear can often be a barrier to being honest because people may be afraid of the potential negative consequences of telling the truth, such as losing relationships, facing judgment, or experiencing repercussions for their actions; however, overcoming that fear and choosing honesty can lead to stronger relationships and a clearer conscience. Similarly, potential whistleblowers may fear retaliation for exposing wrongdoing.

It is interesting to note how, at first, fear creates disorientation and doubt, but over time, it may shift into something that could enhance resilience and unity. As Higgins (2023) pointed out, fear does not necessarily need to be an opposing force. It can be used as a driving force for personal growth and resilience, especially in high-pressure situations. Fear-based environments are confusing, but with strong situational awareness skills – the ability to anticipate and respond effectively to varying circumstances – you can become stronger and develop a methodical way of dealing with problems. This shows how important it is to develop adaptive capacity – a leadership skill that helps people get through tough times and grow.

However, while fear can be a powerful motivator, it has its limits. When used excessively by an egocentric leader, particularly in an evolving workplace culture that prioritizes change and innovation, it can cause more harm than good, stifle creativity, and produce unnecessary levels of anxiety and stress.

Paradoxically, while honesty is generally considered a positive trait in the workplace, it can sometimes boomerang, potentially leading to negative repercussions as unfiltered feedback can sometimes be perceived as harsh or disrespectful, causing tension or unintentionally damaging relationships. Being honest might also lead to defamation or other legal issues if information is shared inappropriately. Lack of transparency, or the presence of a controlling leadership style may not be conducive to open communications with honest opinions, concerns, or criticisms due to fear of retaliation or negative career effects.

EMPATHY

My colleague, research partner, and a healthcare strategy consultant share the following experience involving acquisition negotiations: Senior leadership chose not to share its plans with middle management and staff for fear that the deal could fall through if the information became public during sensitive stages in the negotiation talks. At the same time, many of the hospital system's middle managers had seen positions like theirs become jeopardized when economies of scale opportunities created by acquisitions came to fruition. They wanted to believe that their leadership cared about them.

When the hospital executives finally announced the plan, 10 days prior to the contract signing, many middle managers were disheartened and angry. They believed they were entitled to hear such potentially consequential news far earlier, that they should have been informed not just about the acquisition but about what the acquisition might mean in terms of their positions. They came to believe that the lack of transparency signaled that leadership cared more about the acquisition prospects than about their livelihoods.

Senior executives, on the other hand, believed that they were indeed forthcoming, as evidenced by their contention that the announcement was made as soon as assurances were in place that the merger deal was solidified. In this case, each group viewed transparency quite differently. And each group believed they were not understood and that the other side was short on empathy.

The larger issue, as my colleague came to understand, was that a foundation of transparency and empathy had not been in place. Senior executives and middle managers were separated by perceptions. Each administrative level looked at the timeframe of the announcement, not to mention the lack of consultation with middle management about the merger plan, and saw something quite different: for senior executives, it reaffirmed their unwarranted belief that middle managers would be satisfied with their handling of the issue; for middle management, it signaled a lack of concern about their welfare. It made them feel their interests were not paramount in the minds of senior management, that senior executives did not know what it was like to walk in their shoes. For middle managers, this failure to be heard was, at heart, a matter of trust.

The ndiation in this case would not have been to jeopardize the merger deal by announcing it prematurely. Had the news been leaked, even inadvertently, it could have derailed the merger since other hospitals had been vying quite competitively for becoming part of the hospital system. But had a culture of trust been in place, middle managers would have been more understanding of the need to keep the deal under wraps. Trustworthiness, the foundation of honesty and transparency, thus, may be viewed as a perception contextualized by climate. If employees and other stakeholders believe that openness is a valued dimension of the work life experience, and if such openness is part of a commitment to a culture of trust – and, in this case, if employees had a history of believing that senior leadership always had their interests in mind – they will be far more understanding and forgiving when circumstances arise in which it would be necessary to suspend transparency for the greater good (Eisenberg, 2024).

When employees fear being reprimanded, they may bypass safety protocols or rush through tasks, which can have serious consequences. A fearful environment may also reduce open communication and limit opportunities for creative problem solving, crucial for addressing potential risks during disruptions before they escalate. According to Chamorro-Premuzic (2020), leaders with erratic behaviors, uncontrollable emotions, or a pessimistic worldview might inadvertently stress out their employees using negative or disrespectful language. This may also lead to a toxic work climate where employees feel unsafe or unsupported, contributing to higher anxiety levels and repeated errors.

Fear-based environments that replace persuasion with intimidation and that promote self-interest over empathy and honesty, breed mistrust, and dishonesty in organizations. Lack of humility and poor self-control (or self-regulation) may unleash an unintended consequence of fueling the atmosphere with toxicity. An unintended consequence is the vicious cycle of errors when a series of mistakes or failures reinforce each other, creating a negative feedback loop with reoccurring errors down the line, making the initial problem worse and perpetuating the cycle without a clear way to break free.

A healthy balance of control and autonomy ensures that employees are kept motivated without making them anxious or discouraging them from taking risks and gaining positive experience. Trustworthy leaders create learning spaces that are psychologically safe where employees are supported instead of punished for mistakes, fostering trust and open communication (Sinek, 2011).

When employees feel safe, they are more likely to express concerns, take calculated risks, and perform their best. A safe environment allows employees to emulate the leader's behaviors by being authentic and honest, share ideas without fear of judgment, and engage in innovation and cocreation (Belasen & Pfeffermann, 2024). When leaders are authentically honest at work, they can expect employees to join in the action with enhanced problem-solving communication and idea generation and show a stronger bond and genuine connection with brand identity.

Being Authentically Honest

Building trust by encouraging leaders to demonstrate high levels of personal integrity, especially by being authentically honest, has emerged as the gold standard advice, despite logical and ethical tensions that often require binary choices between staying true to yourself or going with the flow. When leaders balance vulnerability with strength, it reflects high commitment to being authentically honest.

Authenticity is a dynamic process that evolves through constant self-reflection, introspection, and a readiness to grow and learn through applied learning experiences. Leaders must traverse the tensions between their espoused values and actual behaviors by experimenting with new (widely acceptable) pathways that over time allow them to self-understand their genuine leadership style better while also adapting successfully to different situations. Authentically honest leaders are challenged to remain true to themselves while also adapting and evolving as leaders to meet the demands of different situations and cultural contexts.

Being authentically honest at work means having strong self-awareness. It is about knowing your values, emotions, and competencies and how you are perceived by others and expressing opinions and suggestions sensibly while staying honest and truthful to ethical standards within the workplace. This is also a moral duty for leaders – to act with integrity, uphold ethical standards, and prioritize the well-being and fairness of followers or affected stakeholders by making choices considerate of the greater good. Trustworthy leaders strive to do what is right, even in difficult situations, and set a positive example for others to follow throughout the organization.

Effective leader–follower relationships depend on trust because it makes it possible for people to be sincere and forge solid bonds based on common values. By acting on their self-awareness, leading with their hearts as well as their heads and consistently measuring up to their values, authentic leaders foster trust. People trust leaders who are authentic, not copycats, which is why ethics and honesty are crucial in leader–follower relationships. People can tell when a leader is trying to mimic another person's style. Being transparent and vulnerable is another way that leaders foster trust. Leaders can foster a more compassionate and trustworthy atmosphere when they are open about their challenges and mistakes.

The life story and experiences of a leader are the foundation of authenticity. Leaders can be more authentic when they are aware of their life stories and the values that have influenced them. By living up to their beliefs and ideals, leaders gain the trust of others. Leaders can discover what matters most to them and create guiding principles when their values are put to the test. It is also important to be consistent in applying ethical standards in actions and decisions as it further solidifies trust and credibility with followers.

Leaders who consistently act in line with their stated values and ethical commitments, know how to listen actively to their employees, give and receive feedback. These leaders create a positive work climate that not only prioritizes mutual respect, honesty, and accountability but also deepens their authenticity and commitment to adaptability and growth.

Being authentically honest also creates space for imposters who use authenticity as an "excuse for sticking with what's comfortable" because it focuses on the self as a medium that changes while promoting the idea that one can still be authentic (Ibarra, 2015). This raises the question of whether choosing the chameleon route to fit better within the team and learn skills from others even though it may feel unauthentic, at least at first (as it could trigger general nervousness or discomfort that may affect self-perceptions of true self), is a good thing.

After all, breaking outside the comfort zone using the chameleon style of leadership reflects adaptability, with leaders adjusting their approaches to align with specific situations implying that authenticity and adaptability can coexist and reinforce or strengthen the true self. Sometimes, however, it is important to cultivate one's own self-confidence to achieve an unwavering sense of an adaptive self.

DISCOVER YOUR AUTHENTIC LEADERSHIP

Your True North represents who you are as a human being at your deepest level. It is your orienting point – your fixed point in a spinning world – that helps you stay on track as a leader. Your True North is based on your most cherished values, your passions and motivations, and the sources of satisfaction in your life. When you follow your True North, your leadership will be authentic, and people will naturally want to associate with you (George, 2007).

Scholars argued that authentic leadership is a gendered representation of leadership (Hopkins & O'Neil, 2015) due to perceived incongruity – a double-bind dilemma which forces women to make a choice between acting in concert with gender-normative behaviors or with expected leadership role behaviors. Being authentic in organizations that require women to fit into male-dominated contexts puts added pressures on women who struggle with imposter syndrome and who are at risk of missing out on leadership opportunities, the focus of the next section.

Gender in the Middle

Creating a work environment where everyone, regardless of their gender, feels comfortable being truthful and expressing their ideas openly, fostering a culture of transparency and honesty where diverse perspectives are valued and heard without fear is not only critical for building trust, but also vital for organizational performance. However, women middle managers are not fully understood, their authenticity is not acknowledged or valued, and the so-called "female qualities" of relationship and organizational skills are seen as more important for lower levels of the managerial hierarchy.

Women middle managers have a collaborative, more communal way of making tough decisions. They tend to be less abrupt or harsh when trying to obtain "buy in" from frontline leaders. They have eloquent ways of driving their points across and getting employees to take on difficult tasks without appearing demanding or overbearing. Women leaders have the capacity to be more balanced and generally seek out win–win solutions in their decision-making. They explore the causes and consequences of decisions collaboratively and consider their potential impact on affected employees, customers, and shareholders (Belasen & Frank, 2012).

Women middle managers tend to look at details to create a bigger, more holistic picture of a situation before planning. Men, on the other hand, tend to gather as much information as women, but analyze it in a more linear path. Indeed, women scored higher on personality traits associated with conscientiousness (Belasen & Frank, 2008).

Traits like emotional intelligence, empathy, and compassion have been found to be more prevalent in women. Women also seem to regard ethics and integrity at a higher level than men, with women being less accepting than men of dishonest and deceitful tactics (Belasen, 2012). Women middle managers are more likely than men to engage in conversations, elicit opinions, and seek to better understand how their superiors, peers, and subordinates would feel about their attempts at influence.

Women are perceived less favorably than men in promotion opportunities to senior executive positions when their behaviors are perceived to be incongruent with prevailing gender expectations. For example, responses to apologies made by CEOs during major disruptions differed based on the gender of the CEO. Consumers reacted more favorably to denial responses delivered by male CEOs, primarily due to the negative expectancy violation for female CEOs. Such violations resulted in lower trust and less willingness to do business with women-led organizations (Montgomery & Cowen, 2020).

Another study found that men got a greater share of the critical assignments that led to advancement than women did. On average the men's projects had budgets twice as big and were staffed three times greater than the women's. Only 22% of the women, but 30% of the men, were given budgets of more than $10 million, and just 46% of the women, versus 56% of the men received profit and loss (P&L) responsibility (Folkman, 2013). Other research showed that women leaders were found to have greater transformational leadership qualities, espouse ethics and integrity, and manifest a balance of transactional and organizational skills more so than do men (Belasen & Frank, 2008).

More recently, Zenger and Folkman (2020) found that female leaders were more favorably rated by direct reports on 13 of 19 leadership competencies during the COVID-19 Pandemic. Interpersonal skills such as "inspires and motivates," "communicates powerfully," "collaboration/teamwork," and "relationship building" were ranked highly and women ranked highest on all of these.

Women leaders have the capacity to be more balanced and pursue win–win solutions in decisions and outcomes that affect employees, customers, and shareholders. This big-picture thinking may help women to deal more successfully with ambiguity in complex business settings. Women demonstrate social skills and experiences in interpersonal relationships, and participative decision-making (Hsu et al., 2022), essential for building or restoring trust during disruption (Post et al., 2019).

Gender and Honesty

Perceptions of trustworthiness may be complicated by the fact that some variables may exist without others. Behavioral measures in experimental settings are often tied to a specific context and are considered indirect measures of trust because it is possible to engage in trust-related behaviors without often involving trust (Chiou & Lee, 2021). For example, a leader may be honest but be perceived as not credible or not worthy of trust. On the other hand, survey methods (i.e., self-report) represent direct measures of trust, because trust is fundamentally an attitude and not a behavior (Alsaid et al., 2023). Respondents reflect on their attitudes and closely held beliefs and expectations that are important for understanding how they perceive trust.

Previous studies with self-reports showed that female middle managers have greater transformational leadership qualities, espouse ethics and integrity, and display a balance of leadership skills and personality traits more so than do men (Belasen and Frank, 2012). More recently, Belasen & Belasen (2025) showed that on average women described their actual traits of transparency, credibility, and accountability lower than the men did. However, women described their honesty higher than men did. For both genders, honesty was also the highest rated trait overall, both in the respondents' self-measure and in their reflected level of desirability (Figure 7.1). Both genders rated their own transparency as their lowest scoring trait and treated it as the least important of the desired traits (Figure 7.2).

The results illustrate that women differ from men on the characteristics of trustworthy leadership. Of utmost importance is the difference in honesty where women self-reported higher levels of honesty than did men. The high desirability scores may provide clues that women not only aspire to greater levels of honesty, but they appear to value it highly in their leadership behavior. These results are quite revealing considering

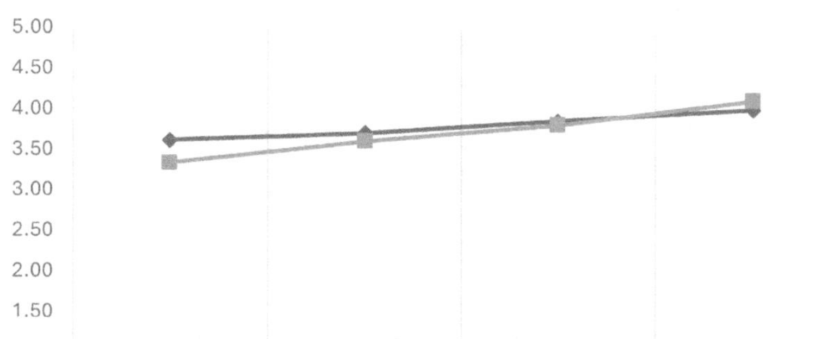

	TRANSPARENCY	CREDIBILITY	ACCOUNTABILITY	HONESTY
Actual M	3.61	3.70	3.85	3.99
Actual F	3.33	3.6	3.8	4.1

Figure 7.1 Self-Reported Ratings – Actual Traits

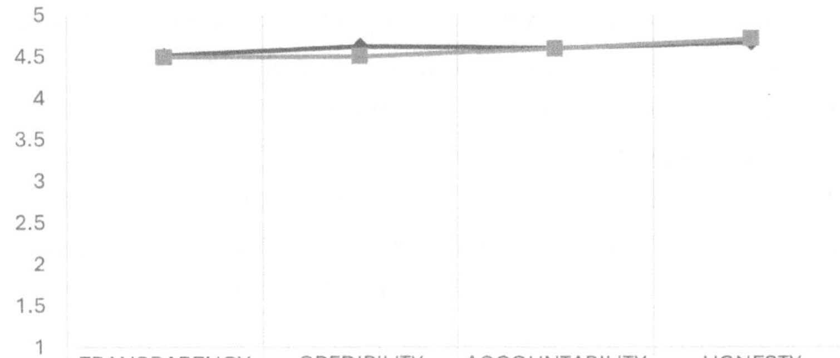

	TRANSPARENCY	CREDIBILITY	ACCOUNTABILITY	HONESTY
Desired M	4.51	4.62	4.6	4.67
Desired F	4.49	4.5	4.59	4.71

Figure 7.2 Self-Reported Ratings – Desired Traits

that men and women in leadership positions tend to rate their abilities and qualities quite similarly (Sturm et al., 2014).

Becoming Intrinsically Honest

Honesty is crucial for middle managers as they act as a bridge between senior leadership and frontline leaders, requiring them to be transparent in communicating information upward and downward, while also upholding ethical standards within their teams, even when faced with the pressure to deliver results. When middle managers are honest with their teams, it builds trust and loyalty, leading to increased employee engagement and productivity. Honest communication promotes collaborative behavior and enables open feedback loops, where employees feel comfortable sharing concerns and providing input to their managers.

Middle managers often face situations where they need to make tough decisions, especially in conflicting situations where balancing honesty with the need to maintain team harmony can be challenging. Demonstrating honesty in their own behavior, however, encourages similar behavior from their direct reports. It also ensures that middle managers prioritize ethical conduct over personal gain. This can be done with strong self-regulation and ethical mindfulness. Mindful leaders do not think in exclusive, binary terms.

Often, mutually exclusive categories are the cause of leadership failure. Instead, mindful leaders use reframing skills that bring into view the elements of the process and the ability to correct any deviations that may be out of place. Effective middle managers display behavioral flexibility that allows them to master contradictory behaviors while also keep some measure of behavioral integrity and credibility. Furthermore, when middle managers show vulnerability, they set a strong example that inspires frontline leaders to fully engage their teams, embrace learning and continuous improvement, and make their contributions more meaningful to the organization.

FOSTERING A CULTURE OF VULNERABILITY

In an era where the boundary between work and personal life is increasingly blurred, navigating personal story sharing demands a nuanced approach. For workers, sharing the personal story remains essential to their well-being and success, but requires an intentional and strategic approach. The way forward for leaders involves dismantling workplace paradigms that penalize some individuals for sharing with vulnerability. To harness the power of storytelling in the workplace, we must work toward eliminating structures that only favor some for sharing authentically. By dismantling these barriers, we pave the way for a more inclusive and empowering environment where the experiences of all individuals are valued and celebrated (Woolf, 2024).

Ethical mindfulness becomes a form of self-regulation that causes one to behave with higher levels of personal integrity and honesty – with the presence of ethical consciousness from one decision or behavioral event to another. Self-regulation is associated with insistence toward accomplishing goals and diligence in mitigating efforts that inhibit or hinder the achievement of goals. When organizational members interact with trustworthy leaders who display self-regulation, they also perceive them as ethical and honest and are motivated to emulate such behaviors.

While ethical and authentic leaders build trust and inspire high commitment, acting with empathy allows leaders to connect more deeply with their followers' perspectives and needs, enhancing overall morale and inclusivity within the organization. Empathy ensures that ethical decisions not only align with core values but also consider the impact on employees' well-being.

Empathetic decision-making encourages leaders to think beyond policies and protocols, allowing for more nuanced, person-centered leadership that resonates with followers on a personal level. Indra Nooyi exemplified this by showing genuine concern for her employees' welfare, which made her strategic vision more relatable and meaningful to those involved. Empathy, combined with trust and ethics, cultivates a more resilient organizational culture where employees feel seen, heard, and appreciated (Madden, 2024).

It is vital for senior executives and HR directors to establish clear organizational values and ethical guidelines that are consistently communicated to all levels. To sustain the leadership development pipeline, they could initiate targeted leadership development programs for middle managers which also include skills for navigating ethical choices and promoting open communication. Equally important is creating safe spaces for middle managers to raise concerns and provide feedback without fear of reprisal.

AI and Middle Managers

AI algorithms can efficiently analyze data and offer forecasts and implementation options that were previously considered to be within the prerogatives of middle managers, leading to fear of job displacement. This fear has been further exacerbated by a lack of transparency about how AI is used in reaching conclusions and the potential for built-in biases within the algorithms leading to outcomes that middle managers may be held accountable for.

THE POSSIBILITY FOR REPLACEMENT

Artificial Intelligence has been garnering headlines and is the talk of the town in a corporate setup. While some are excited to witness how it will evolve the job market, others are apprehensive that it might take away their roles. After witnessing the immense capability this emerging technology possesses, a critical question has surfaced in the minds of most working professionals: Will I be replaced by AI? No wonder, artificial intelligence is performing miracles in cubicles, there are certain areas where human skills are leading the charts. Be it a friend or a foe, the truth is AI is going to prevail and become stronger in the coming years. Can it take our jobs? Yes.

A striking report by Gartner, a research and consulting firm that assists businesses to utilize technology to enhance their performance, unearths a shocking revelation that by 2026, 50% of middle management roles will be cut off and substituted by AI in 20% of companies. Such statistics can be unsettling, but they underscore the urgent need for professionals to adapt. The key to surviving in the evolving world is to learn to coexist with this not-so-welcome guest (Tewari, 2024).

AI technology facilitates both centralization and decentralization of the supervision structure in organizations, necessitating a drastic change on how middle managers perform their leadership roles. The need for honesty and transparency in the use of information drives middle managers to explore new ways to preserve their value proposition. HR and IT support staff have a role in facilitating the transition from traditional to hybrid working environments, alleviating concerns about the algorithms and building trust. They guide middle managers on how AI works, its strengths and limitations, and how to interpret outcomes ensuring that AI tools are designed with ethical considerations in mind, mitigating potential biases and promoting fairness in decision-making.

Middle managers can also take an active role in redefining their tasks and responsibilities, propose and lead AI development and implementation projects, create new workflows that leverage human talents and AI capabilities and that demonstrate value beyond traditional middle management tasks. These initiatives may boost the credibility of middle managers and inspire their ownership and renewed commitment to building a personal brand around innovative digitally focused leadership.

Padisetti (2024), Forbes Councils member, offers the following guidelines for reimagining the role of middle managers in the new AI era including

1. shifting the focus from communication conduits to becoming insight architects by helping to integrate AI-generated tools in communications and best practices; transforming quantitative insights into qualitative strategic advantages;
2. mastering the human-AI collaboration interface by translating executive vision into feasible AI frameworks; identifying AI-driven versus human-led tasks; and creating

seamless workflows that maximize both human talents and AI capabilities;
3. sustaining human capital skills including stakeholder management, cultural intelligence, and empathy; creative problem-solving in ambiguous situations; building trust, honesty, and psychological safety in teams.

While implementation strategies are prioritized differently by executives and middle managers, they may include an honest self-audit of the middle managers' current roles, jointly identifying tasks that could be automated; supporting middle managers' knowledge development in AI tools and platforms; building strong cross-functional relationships that technology cannot be easily imitated or replaced; and identifying critical business problems that require human judgment and EI, not AI, skills.

THE NEW VALUE PROPOSITION

Managers who excel in these three areas become indispensable to their organizations, even as AI capabilities expand. These aren't theoretical constructs – they're battle-tested elements that consistently differentiate high-performing middle managers in the AI era.

Successful middle managers must reframe their value proposition around three core elements:

1. **Strategic Integration**
   - Connect organizational silos that AI systems can't bridge.
   - Identify strategic opportunities that emerge from AI-generated insights.
   - Transform data into actionable business strategies.
2. **Human Capital Development**
   - Coach teams through AI-driven transformation.
   - Build resilient, adaptable team cultures.
   - Develop human capabilities that complement AI systems.

3. **Innovation Catalyst**
   - Identify new business opportunities arising from AI implementation.
   - Create novel solutions that combine human creativity with AI capabilities.
   - Drive organizational evolution beyond simple automation (Padisetti, 2024).

It is increasingly essential to reconcile the competing tensions inherent in digital transformations (e.g., change vs. stability). As middle managers navigate these tensions, they are advised to adapt their approaches to accommodate the evolving landscape of work, harness technology, and foster a culture of collaborative innovation. Embracing the paradoxes and deploying adaptive leadership styles help prioritize staying abreast of emerging technologies and innovative solutions while fostering a culture of trust.

In doing so, middle managers can position their organizations for success, playing a pivotal role by ensuring frontline readiness to confront the dynamic challenges and opportunities of AI integration. To achieve this goal effectively, they create robust processes and adaptive systems, paving the way for sustainable growth of the organization within the industry.

The Competitive Advantage of Honesty

Psychologically safe workplaces are characterized by a strong adherence to higher levels of trust and commitment to the goals of diversity. McKinsey (2020), for example, shows that companies in the top 25% for inclusion and gender diversity were, respectively, 36% and 25% more likely to have superior financial returns. Gender diversity in middle management was also found to be a strategic resource that provides a sustainable competitive advantage by creating value that cannot be easily or quickly imitated by competitors. Business firms with balanced diversity (between 40% and 60% women as employees) at the middle management and staff levels tend to be more profitable (Ferrary & Déo, 2022). Experiments show that when honesty is fully transparent in organizations, it can provide a competitive advantage. Honest firms sell more and, despite higher costs (vs. perceived dishonest competitors), achieve higher profits (Pigors & Rockenbach, 2016).

Diverse leadership is a cultural intelligence competency, the foundation upon which adaptability, honesty, and mutual respect thrive. Strong perceptions of honesty allow middle managers to stand out by presenting themselves as more reliable and genuine in communicating or influencing others.

Middle managers' familiarity with the workings of the organization and their proximity to decision makers make their "clutch roles" during transitions critical for organizational success. They search for new opportunities, align strategies and operational activities, evaluate the merits of strategy execution, and propose new projects. The duality of having strategic awareness with operating experience often requires ambidextrous skills to manage current operations while at the same time exploring new venues essential for sustaining disruptive change.

The concept of sliding up (governance role) and down (advocacy role) was used by Hales (2006) to describe how middle managers move between managerial activities to employee advocacy roles. Down the hierarchy, they should demonstrate a willingness to share power by creating meaningful opportunities for staff involvement as well as taking an active interest in their career development. Regaining employees' trust after disappointing experiences can become quite challenging, especially during transitions. Demonstrating honesty by shifting the focus to influencing processes and decisions, not controlling them is vital for facilitating an understanding between senior executives and middle managers as well as increasing reputation.

Businesses build their differentiated brand strategy from the inside-out by projecting unique attributes of high-performance to their consumers and ensuring customer loyalty. When senior executives and middle managers develop and sustain a culture of high performance, they also enhance the organization's perceived reputation, as it indicates a strong commitment to excellence, employee satisfaction, and positive results, which are key factors that stakeholders consider when evaluating a company's trustworthiness, honesty, and reliability.

High-performance culture is seen as a sign of a well-managed, reliable organization that delivers consistent quality and value to customers, investors, and stakeholders. The reputation of a business largely relies on its corporate reputation and entails the evaluation by consumers of the honesty and expertise of that business. Trust is essential in the relationship between sellers and buyers or businesses and their partners. The business reputation is significantly influenced by perceptions of honesty, when partners and customers view the business as credible, trustworthy, and honest.

Conclusion

Trustworthy and honest middle managers possess leadership qualities that make them stand out as leaders with strong integrity, honesty, confidence, and resilience. Leaders who can effectively communicate their vision, inspire trust through ethical behavior, and empower their team to achieve goals while navigating challenges. Confidence nurtures the capacity to bounce back quickly from challenges or unexpected disruptions. As resilience develops, every display of honesty contributes to heightened confidence in and around the organization. Leadership is not just about having a position of authority or holding a title; it is about the ability to remain authentically honest, guide, and empower others.

The influence of trustworthy leaders goes beyond just achieving bottom line results. Trustworthiness is the foundation upon which successful relationships are built. When teams and frontline employees are consistently exposed to middle managers they trust, particularly those who exhibit a strong sense of ethical behavior and honesty, they tend to assimilate and replicate these behaviors, collaborating and achieving mutually beneficial solutions. Being truthful, honest, and transparent in decisions and actions is fundamental to achieving positive results, as it builds trust, fosters open communication, and strengthens relationships up and down organizational lines.

References

Alsaid, A., Li, M., Chiou, E. K., & Lee, J. D. (2023). Measuring trust: A text analysis approach to compare, contrast, and select trust questionnaires. *Frontiers in Psychology*, 14, 1192020.

Belasen, A. (2012). *Developing Women Leaders in Corporate America, Balancing Competing Demands, Transcending Traditional Boundaries.* Santa Barbara, CA, Praeger.

Belasen, A. T., & Belasen, A. R. (2025). Signaling trust during disruptions: perceived gender differences in trustworthy leadership traits. *Gender in Management: An International Journal.* https://doi.org/10.1108/GM-04-2024-0187.

Belasen, A., & Frank, N. M. (2008). Competing values leadership: Quadrant roles and personality traits. *Leadership and Organizational Development Journal*, 29(2), 127–143.

Belasen, A., & Frank, N. M. (2012). Using the competing values framework to evaluate the interactive effects of gender and personality traits on leadership roles. *The International Journal of Leadership Studies,* 7(2), 192–215.

Belasen, A., & Pfeffermann, N. (2024). *Brilliant Leadership – Unlocking the Power of Innovation-Communication*. New York, NY, Routledge.

Bennis, W., & Thomas, R. J. (2002). Crucibles of leadership. *Harvard Business Review,* 80(9), 39–45. https://hbr.org/2002/09/crucibles-of-leadership.

Chamorro-Premuzic, T. (2020, May 11). 5 ways leaders accidentally stress out their employees. *Harvard Business Review.* https://hbr.org/2020/05/5-ways-leaders-accidentally-stress-out-their-employees.

Chiou, E. K., & Lee, J. D. (2021). Trusting automation: Designing for responsivity and resilience. *Human Factors,* 65, 137–165.

Deloitte Global Human Capital Trends. (2019). Retrieved from https://www2.deloitte.com/za/en/pages/human-capital/articles/2019-deloitte-global-human-capital-trends-.html.

Eisenberg, B. (2024). The convergence of empathy and authenticity in brilliant leadership. chapter 2, in Alan T Belasen & Nicole Pfeffermann (Eds.), *Brilliant Leadership – Unlocking the Power of Innovation-Communication*, pp. 23–41, New York, NY, Routledge.

Ferrary, M., & Déo, S. (2022). Gender diversity and firm performance: When diversity at middle management and staff levels matter. *The International Journal of Human Resource Management*, 34(14), 2797–2831. https://doi.org/10.1080/09585192.2022.2093121.

Folkman, Z. (2013). Women in the workplace: A research roundup. *Harvard Business Review*, September. https://hbr.org/2013/09/women-in-the-workplace-a-research-roundup.

George, B. (2007). True North: Discover your authentic leadership, March 28. https://billgeorge.org/article/true-north-discover-your-authentic-leadership/.

Hales, C. (2006). Moving down the line? The shifting boundary between middle and first-line management. *Journal of General Management*, 32(2), 31–55. https://doi.org/10.1177/030630700603200203.

Higgins, M. (2023). Don't let fear hold you back — use it to push you forward. *Harvard Business Review,* June 19. https://hbr.org/2023/06/I-let-fear-hold-you-back-use-it-to-push-you-forward.

Hopkins, M. M., & O'Neil, D. A. (2015). Authentic leadership: Application to women leaders. *Frontiers in Psychology*, 6, 959. https://doi.org/10.3389/fpsyg.2015.00959.

Hsu, N., Newman, D. A., & Badura, K. L. (2022). Emotional intelligence and transformational leadership: Meta-analysis and explanatory model of female leadership advantage. *Journal of Intelligence*, 10(4), 104. https://doi.org/10.3390/jintelligence10040104.

Ibarra, H. (2015). The authenticity paradox. *Harvard Business Review*, 93(1–2), 52–59. ISSN 0017-8012.

Kennedy, J. A., & Kray, L. J. (2022). Gender similarities and differences in dishonesty. *Current Opinion in Psychology*, 48, 101461. https://doi.org/10.1016/j.copsyc.2022.101461.

Madden, K. (2024). Leading with empathy: A path to exceptional leadership, October 14. https://www.forbes.com/councils/forbescoachescouncil/2024/10/14/leading-with-empathy-a-path-to-exceptional-leadership/.

McKinsey. (2020). Diversity wins: How inclusion matters, May 19. https://www.mckinsey.com/featured-insights/diversity-and-inclusion/diversity-wins-how-inclusion-matters.

Montgomery, N. V., & Cowen, A. P. (2020). How leader's gender influences external audience response to organizational failures. *Journal of Personality and Social Psychology*, 118(4), 639–660. https://doi.org/10.1037/pspa0000176.

Padisetti, M. (2024). Reimagining middle management in the era of AI, November 27. https://www.forbes.com/councils/forbestechcouncil/2024/11/27/reimagining-middle-management-in-the-era-of-ai/.

Pigors, M., & Rockenbach, B. (2016). The competitive advantage of honesty. *European Economic Review*, 891, 407–424.

Post, C., Latu, I. M., & Belkin, L. Y. (2019). A female leadership trust advantage in times of crisis: Under what conditions? *Psychology of Women Quarterly*, 43(2), 215–231.

Rooke, D., & Torbert, W. R. (2005). Seven transformations of leadership. *Harvard Business Review*, 83(4), 68–76. https://hbr.org/2005/04/seven-transformations-of-leadership.

Sinek, S. (2011). *Start with Why: How Great Leaders Inspire Everyone to Take Action*. New York, Portfolio/Penguin.

Sturm, R. E., Taylor, S. N., Atwater, L. E., & Braddy, P. W. (2014). Leader self-awareness: An examination and implications of women's under-prediction, *Journal of Organizational Behavior,* 35(5), 657–677.

Tewari, T. (2024). 50% of middle management roles to be replaced by AI in 20% of companies by 2026. *TQI Education*, October 25. https://timesofindia.indiatimes.com/education/news/.

Vogelgesang Lester, G., Clapp-Smith, R., & Palmer, N. (2009). The role of authentic leadership and cultural intelligence in cross-cultural contexts: An objectivist perspective. *International Journal of Leadership Studies*, 5(2), 102–117.

Woodman, P. (2016). Boosting trust in your middle managers. HR, November 22. https://www.hrmagazine.co.uk/content/features/boosting-trust-in-your-middle-managers/.

Woolf, J. (2024). How Pixar fosters a culture of vulnerability at work. *Harvard Business Review*, March 25. https://hbr.org/2024/03/how-pixar-fosters-a-culture-of-vulnerability-at-work.

Zenger, J., & Folkman, J. (2020, December 30). Research: Women are better leaders during a crisis. *Harvard Business Review*, Product ID H063D0.

Chapter 8

Bridging the Trust Gap, Finding the Middle Ground

Introduction

At times underappreciated, middle managers still play an important role in organizations. Whether through communication linkages or simply by greasing the wheel of productivity, organizations with properly inspired middle managers typically have a stronger core culture and more profitable outcomes. In fact, an analysis by McKinsey (2023) shows that organizations with top-performing middle managers yield multiple times the total shareholder returns (TSR) or capital gains versus those with below par middle managers. In fact, predictions by BLS (2024) show that overall employment in management occupations is projected to grow faster than the average for all occupations from 2023 to 2033.

Yet, many middle managers typically point to the lack of information or poor communication from senior executives, leaving them unsure of what is required of them while

DOI: 10.4324/9781003608028-8

simultaneously needing to support their teams and frontline leaders when harsh policies or decisions are made.

Working closely with middle managers as part of management education and development programs and throughout our own research projects across industries and organizations, we rarely see that a commitment to the organization's strategy is problematic for middle managers. Instead, their concerns involve a lack of untimely communication and limited resources coming from senior executives.

THE TRUTH ABOUT MIDDLE MANAGERS

"Middle management" is a term associated with relentless downsizing, corporate drudgery, and career dead ends. Bashed by management gurus, dismissed by social scientists, and painted as victims by the media, middle managers seem permanently relegated to the sidelines of corporate power. But is this popular picture accurate? Are middle managers no longer valued by today's performance-driven organizations? ...While managers have maintained their commitment to their tasks and to their colleagues, they are increasingly cynical and distant from their organizations. They are confused about their future and how to manage their careers. This comes at a time when the value of middle management is much greater than ever before (Osterman, 2009).

Have middle managers been dethroned as top executives rationalize resources and leadership talent? Are they unfairly blamed or targeted for problems or failures caused by others? Are middle managers sponsored or groomed for senior leadership positions? Insufficient middle-manager development could lead to the risk of burnout, disengagement, and high turnover that could shutter the leadership talent pipeline and undermine succession planning. Higher turnover rates or disengaged (and demoralized!) middle managers might also affect organizational performance due to knowledge gaps, disruption of workflows, and the need for constant recruitment and training that diminish the vital connection between strategy and execution.

Losing middle managers contributes to organizational **brain drain**, when a significant amount of human capital leaves the organization through the loss of knowledge and experience. This is because middle managers often possess essential institutional memory – the deep uncodified knowledge of processes, projects, client relationships, and team dynamics. When they exit the organization, this critical knowledge may be lost, significantly disrupting teams and workflows as well as hindering strategy execution and affecting efficiency and operational effectiveness.

In this chapter, we explore the gap between how executives view middle managers' contributions to the organization, their perceptions of what motivates middle managers, the struggles of middle managers to demonstrate their premium up-and-down the chain of command while being caught between a rock and a hard place, and the unintended consequences of mistrust and the lack of open communication within the context of this gap. We then discuss strategies for building and preserving trust across hierarchical lines, how executives can shift their mindset by recognizing the critical role of middle managers as change catalysts, not bureaucratic bottlenecks, harnessing their strengths, empowering and involving them in strategic decision-making for win–win outcomes.

New Challenges

To meet the new challenges of communication innovation and expansion into open markets, organizations have been instituting reforms and structural changes including team-based design, interprofessional collaboration and shared leadership (Belasen & Rufer, 2013;Belasen & Pfeffermann, 2024). These changes punctuate the critical role of middle managers as strategic communicators, change champions, and facilitators with the know-how to translate high-level goals into actionable plans that frontline leaders and teams can follow.

Zenger and Folkman (2014) examined the demographic characteristics of unhappy employees among more than 320,000 individuals in a variety of organizations and found that 16,000 (5%) were middle managers. The main source of unhappiness included *poor leadership* as the number one reason followed by "no career or promotion opportunities;" "work lacks meaning and purpose;" "being treated unfairly compared with others;" "feeling under-appreciated;" "being overworked;" and "viewing the organization as inefficient and ineffective." For organizations with narrow profit margins, turning that 5% around could have a dramatic effect on the bottom line – especially since 48% of the middle managers reportedly considered leaving their current jobs in two years or less (McKinney et al., 2013).

A decade later, Gallup (2024) found two aspects of leadership that make a significant difference in how people feel about disruptive change: **trust and communication.** Employees in organizations with trustworthy leaders were 4.5 times as likely to be engaged and 62% less likely to feel burned out at work. Among those same disrupted employees, those who strongly agreed their leaders communicate effectively with the rest of their organization saw similar benefits. They were 4.3 times as likely to be engaged and 65% less likely to feel frequently burned out at work.

Leaders and managers are more likely to experience extensive disruptive changes in their roles. Over half of the managers surveyed by Gallup (2024) stated their organization has restructured teams, while nearly half say they have had to make budget cuts. This means more work with tighter budgets and new teams working in different ways and requiring different methods of management or leadership skills. Gallup research pointed out that middle managers are crucial for company success and employee engagement, with their abilities and skills significantly affecting 70% of the variance in team performance. Without much support from senior executives, feeling demoralized, 43% of these managers reported high levels of burnout and stress. Gallup's research shows that middle managers are facing a "squeeze" with more work, tighter budgets, and new teams, and are at greater risk of job loss during company layoffs.

Confirming the findings by Letian (2023), Gallup (2024) highlighted the importance of managers acting as coaches, leaders, and developers, reinforcing the need for organizations to invest in developing these skills in middle managers so they can effectively inspire and guide their teams.

Becoming Hypereffective

Conscious about the likelihood of being eliminated, demoted, or bypassed, surviving or hopeful middle managers attempt to "prove their premium" by working excessively hard, becoming hypereffective, a behavioral response which was pervasive during the downsizing waves in the 1990s (Belasen & Frank, 2004).

Pressure to increase hours at work comes from the need to perform their roles better but also from the need to pick up the slack left by less engaged managers or were let go. On the surface, hypereffective managers appear more productive and with added motivation to commit to organizational goals. However, a great deal of personal time is traded to maintain or achieve the goals of the organization. There is a competing tension in that hypereffective managers find fewer opportunities to diminish performance in some areas to increase their attention in other areas.

Hypereffectivity may sound good as it tends to transform middle managers into conservative and overworked managers who are pushed to the limits by the expectations of those above them who demand nothing short of better results. With proper support from senior executives, these overworked managers can display a positive work climate by empowering their teams to achieve goals, ultimately leading to increased overall output and efficiency as well as enabling team members to take ownership and develop their skills. When senior executives acknowledge and celebrate the contributions of middle managers, they also reinforce positive behaviors and create a sense of appreciation, boosting managers' morale and leading to increased productivity and job satisfaction.

However, the pattern of change in the tasks and responsibilities underlying the roles performed by hypereffective managers suggests a severe loss of discretionary time and an increase in the sense of powerlessness, or feeling helpless, potentially leading to negative mental and physical health consequences. Surviving middle managers work longer hours with greater responsibilities that require monitoring, not necessarily decision-making.

Being overlooked by senior executives who prioritize developing high-potential leaders for senior leadership roles while neglecting the needs of middle managers who are crucial for day-to-day operations, middle managers often resort to disengagement and avoidance. Research shows that while executives understand the importance of grooming the next successor, they do not see this as an urgent matter (Belasen & Belasen, 2016). Meanwhile, overburdened, and undertrained middle managers are typically on the verge of burning out, while at the same time they are being considered for fewer senior leadership roles.

Squeezed Middle

Having the stressful task of absorbing the discontent of upper and lower levels and without decision making authority, middle managers tend to internalize failure and consequently suffer higher rates of depressive symptoms and anxiety than those at the top or bottom. Researchers at Columbia University found that 18% of supervisors and managers reported symptoms of depression, primarily due to their discontent stemming from spending too much time on administrative tasks and routine meetings, leaving them little time for leading (Prins et al., 2015).

Middle managers are expected to impose decisions formulated by senior executives – ones they did not develop – on subordinates who might object to those new directions. They feel increasingly isolated from senior executives, lose confidence in their judgmental abilities and, uncertain about their future, respond by shifting personal commitments. It is the diminished role in decision-making, the freedom to determine "how to get there," the making of the decision, not the execution, that is demoralizing.

THE SQUEEZE IS REAL: WHAT'S CAUSING IT?

When Gallup asked managers what changes their organization made in 2023, **64%** said "employees were given additional job responsibilities," **51%** cited the "restructuring of teams" and **42%** reported "budget cuts." In short, managers now have *more work to do* on a *tighter budget* with *new teams.*

To make matters worse, Gallup's most recent survey of Fortune 500 CHROs found that "middle managers" are at the greatest risk of losing their jobs, within companies undergoing layoffs in 2023. This means the remaining managers will likely be leading larger teams (Gallup, 2023a).

Surprisingly, however, executives who react harshly to these attitudes and behaviors also typecast middle managers as being unmotivated and therefore being bypassed and otherwise incentivized monetarily to accomplish important tasks (Belasen & Belasen, 2017). Bypassing middle managers, or "layer skipping," involves executives who engage directly with frontline leaders, which can offer quicker access to frontline insights but also create challenges for the undermined middle managers.

The combination of greater executive span with less hierarchical depth creates a dual effect of narrow expertise or de-skilling and a decrease in managerial autonomy with adverse effects on middle managers' morale, turnover rates, and performance. A related effect that was noted in Chapter 3 is the problem of the Pygmalion effect and the perceived lack of commitment and motivation on the part of middle managers. Senior executives believe that middle managers are less motivated to perform their tasks and therefore require greater external regulation (see next section).

However, senior executives can do more to loosen the "squeeze" on middle managers. The Gallup (2023a) report suggested four areas of focus:

- *Promote leadership communication.* Improve the flow of downward and upward communication by giving and receiving timely feedback.

- *Invest in training and development.* The move toward a hybrid workplace requires managers to be flexible, tech-savvy, and focused on transparent communication, trust-building, and fostering a sense of inclusion and engagement, regardless of location.
- *Provide coaching.* Senior executives can take the time to coach and guide middle managers, show empathy, build trust, and encourage them to share their experiences. This coaching strategy can help mitigate early signs of burnout and increase retention.
- *Establish a community of shared accountability.* Frequent contact with fellow managers can help enhance collaboration and cocreation, the sharing of best practices, advice, and emotional support. It is the responsibility of leaders to build such communities.

Senior executives can create opportunities to expand middle managers' skills and knowledge through the leadership development pipeline, sponsorship, and active mentoring.

The potential for upward mobility and increased responsibility can be a strong extrinsic and intrinsic motivator for middle managers. Establishing trusting relationships gives middle managers a sense of belonging and feeling valued for their contributions and achievements.

Finding satisfaction in their daily work and the trust they build with their teams is vital for long-term engagement. Working with a high-performing team and being endorsed by sponsor senior executives can significantly boost motivation and engagement. This creates win–win outcomes as highly motivated middle managers, knowledgeable in innovation implementation (Belasen & Luber, 2017), have unique abilities to make a meaningful impact during disruptions and contribute to the overall success of the organization.

Motivational Gap

A few years ago, as part of a research project for the Academy of Management, the authors of this book embarked on a study of the motivational gaps between senior executives and middle managers (Belasen & Belasen, 2017). Our study was based on four factors of motivation:

1. *Intrinsic motivation* – you do it because it is interesting, pleasant, fun, or you feel good about it.
2. *Self-regulation* – you do it because you have internalized the need and value of the activity.
3. *External regulation* – you do it because *others* reward, neglect, or punish the activity.
4. *Amotivation* – whether you perform the task, you do not appreciate the reasons or feel there are no good reasons to do it.

We found important perceptual differences between what executives say motivates middle managers versus what middle managers say motivates them (Table 8.1). And yet we can see that these perceptions do not line up well with the self-reported numbers by middle managers. This finding has important implications for training and development as well as for facilitating communication across hierarchical levels. Notably, the effects of the perceived motivational gap on engagement and on building trust across the hierarchy are too significant to ignore.

Middle managers are motivated by a combination of factors, including opportunities for growth, recognition, autonomy, and the ability to make a real impact, as well as intrinsic rewards like job satisfaction and the fulfillment of personal goals. Intrinsically, our research shows that middle managers have confidence, discipline, and commitment to the goals of the organization, and are inspired by their sense of accountability

Table 8.1 What Executives Say Motivates Them and What Motivates Middle Managers

	Intrinsic motivation	*Self-regulation*	*External regulation*	*Amotivation*
What executives say motivates them	4.30	4.82	4.33	1.91
What executives say motivates middle managers	3.50	3.80	5.21	3.25
What middle managers say motivates them	4.48	4.54	4.44	1.88

Source: Belasen and Belasen (2017).

and self-worth (*self-regulation*). They often crave the need to make decisions and lead their teams, feeling empowered (*intrinsic motivation*) to identify and solve problems, drive change, and achieve results. Of course, overworked middle managers should expect bonuses, raises, and other forms of financial incentives (*external regulation*), combined with or often less than intrinsic factors.

We can also draw out implications from research to help executives customize the reward system (extrinsic, intrinsic, or variation) according to the specific context of the task environment. Senior executives must recognize that the social contract with middle managers has been weakened as middle managers are less inclined to trade their efforts and loyalty for reduced compensation, diminished recognition, or tarnished reputation. Executives should not overlook the value that middle managers place on intrinsic factors of motivation such as autonomy and recognition or underestimate the benefit of a well-designed motivational strategy (Belasen & Belasen, 2017).

Extrinsic rewards can potentially diminish the value of intrinsic rewards by creating an environment where organizational members are focused on the reward rather than on the work itself. Extrinsic rewards are also temporary, as they motivate employees to achieve short-term success. Employees whose strengths are recognized display more positive attitudes and are more engaged and effective. Engaged employees support the innovation, growth, and earning potential of their companies.

DISRUPTIVE CHANGE IS HITTING LEADERS AND MANAGERS HARDEST

When Gallup researchers analyzed the differences in performance among business work units, the benefits of **employee engagement** were clear. When comparing employee engagement levels, Gallup found that top- and bottom-quartile business units and teams had the following differences in business outcomes:

81% in absenteeism
58% in patient safety incidents (mortality and falls)
18% in turnover for high-turnover organizations
43% in turnover for low-turnover organizations
28% in shrinkage (theft)
64% in safety incidents (accidents)
41% in quality (defects)
10% in customer loyalty/engagement

18% in productivity (sales)
23% in profitability

These kinds of performance differences are always important to businesses, but they are especially **crucial during disruption**, when an organization's ability to positively affect employee engagement and wellbeing to continue driving growth and productivity is of critical importance.

Another timely benefit of employee engagement in times of uncertainty is that high engagement boosts retention. Employees who are actively engaged are less likely to be actively looking at or open to a new job opportunity. In fact, low engagement teams typically endure turnover rates that are 18%–43% higher than highly engaged teams (Gallup, 2023b).

Middle Managers' Reflections

Over the past few years, we have worked with dozens of middle managers, participating in an MBA in Leadership program focusing on developing leadership skills, communication, organizational management, strategic thinking, and ethical decision-making, integrating theory with practical experience. We asked these managers to share their thoughts and suggestions about motivation at work in general, as well as what motivates them. A selection of their responses is presented below.

Middle Manager 1. Ultimately, blending intrinsic and extrinsic motivators seems to be the way forward. Organizations should think about how to integrate recognition programs that cater to both types of motivation – acknowledging achievements that can resonate with intrinsic desires while financial bonuses appeal to extrinsic ones. So, while intrinsic motivation is getting more attention, especially in flexible environments like Results Only Work Environment (ROWE), I believe it is too soon to say that extrinsic motivation is becoming less important. By fostering an environment that values trust, communication, and accountability while also recognizing the role of extrinsic rewards, organizations can create a motivated workforce that thrives on both internal drive and external recognition.

Middle Manager 2. Firms should take a holistic approach to motivation using both intrinsic and extrinsic variables to create a more engaged and loyal workforce.

Middle Manager 3. Valuing employees can contribute to employee engagement. Employees are likely to become more engaged if their leadership treats them like an asset.

Middle Manager 4. Providing learning and development programs, mentoring, and ways to move up in your career can also boost your own motivation.

Middle Manager 5. Incentives are nice, but a purpose is better. While intrinsic motivation is often more powerful and sustainable than extrinsic motivation, extrinsic motivation will never be completely irrelevant because they provide incentives like pay and benefits. However, the negative aspect of extrinsic motivation is that it can weaken intrinsic motivation by shifting the focus from the activity itself to the reward. Trust and effective communication are essential for building relationships, creating a positive work environment, and ensuring that employees feel valued and supported. Bridging the trust gap will create success..."

Middle Manager 6. Middle managers are the ones who have the power to emotionally support and understand the needs of the lower level employees, and they "act as a resource to first line supervisors," communicating any pain points or areas where we can intrinsically motivate employees better. Middle managers must balance "competing commitments to change and continuity by knowing when to provide structure and direction and when to 'let go' and react to emotional needs." These managers are key to keeping high emotional intelligence in an organization since they interact with the employees in their day to day. By prioritizing the mental health and leadership skills of middle managers, we can help employees overall feel more intrinsically motivated.

Middle Manager 7. In general, a CEO is simply too detached from day-to-day operations to understand the emotions and personal issues that may impact work. Emotional intelligence, or the ability to not only control your own emotions, but the emotions of those around you, has become a vital trait for successful leaders. This concept is largely seen in a middle manager's ability to show empathy with employees. If employees do not feel they are respected or treated fairly they will likely leave. When you have a middle manager with zero EI skills you will find that the employees who have been your top performers for years now are doing the bare minimum and have zero interest in putting any effort into growing the company. These employees almost always blame the lack of supportive middle managers, as the reason for "quiet quitting."

Middle Manager 8. Middle managers are essential for fostering a supportive environment since they interact directly with employees and understand their day-to-day challenges. Middle managers can address the needs of their team while also being a crucial access point between frontline employees and upper management. They can communicate concerns and areas for improvement, helping to create a more intrinsically motivated workforce. Emotional intelligence can empower middle managers at every level to help their teams feel valued and understood.

Middle Manager 9. Results-based work environment (ROWE) is an extrinsic motivator meant to enhance the intrinsic motivation of the employee. It is earned through mutual trust. However, not everyone is cut out to be self-motivated at which time the middle manager needs to recognize the situation and step in. Exercising tough empathy means giving people what they need, not what they want. Now this doesn't necessarily mean revoking the employee's ability to have a flexible work schedule. Assessing the situation, stepping in, and talking with the employee to figure out the root cause can make all the difference in their motivation and success.

Middle Manager 10. Middle managers can also show employees how to do things in a way that will keep them motivated, get more work done, and keep them on the job. Middle managers can use emotional intelligence to help individuals and make virtual spaces that provide emotional support. This helps close the gap that ROWE creates and makes sure that employees still feel connected to the organization's mission, which is a key part of keeping employees motivated.

Middle Manager 11. Leaders who can develop trust and good relationships create an environment conducive to intrinsic drive. Employees who lack trust may feel alienated, which can dramatically diminish their drive. During the early stages of employment, pay and bonuses are frequently used to lure talent. However, once employees settle in, their desire for meaningful work takes precedence. I underscore the importance of middle management in bridging the gap between leaders and employees. Middle managers who can successfully communicate and create trust within their teams have a much better chance of tapping intrinsic motivation. As we negotiate disruptive changes, it is obvious that a hybrid strategy, which includes both internal and extrinsic motivators, will produce the best results. Understanding our teams' different requirements and developing an open communication culture may help us increase engagement and, ultimately, promote corporate success.

Middle Manager 12. Setting high expectations and offering unique incentives can certainly boost morale. However, it is essential to note that a purely extrinsic approach may not sustain long-term engagement, as it could lead to a lack of personal investment in the work. It is essential to recognize that both types of motivation have their place and that a solely extrinsic or intrinsic approach may not be sustainable in the long run. Ultimately, a balanced approach that incorporates both intrinsic and extrinsic motivators may be the key to a highly motivated workforce. By acknowledging individual differences and creating a supportive work environment that values both types of motivation, organizations can foster higher satisfaction and productivity.

Middle Manager 13. As I navigated my career and my role in the Army while pursuing my education, I began to realize that while salary is important, it's not everything. Over time, I started valuing other factors like work schedule, job flexibility, and benefits, which are examples of extrinsic motivations that companies offer to attract employees. However, intrinsic motivation also plays a key role. When I worked as an operations manager at a hospital, although I had a high-paying role with good external rewards, I found myself lacking intrinsic motivation. I didn't feel passionate about the job, and that affected my performance and engagement. I was doing the work but without the drive or satisfaction that comes from enjoying what you do.

Middle Manager 14. I believe the key is to find a balance between both extrinsic and intrinsic motivation. Extrinsic rewards like promotions, higher pay, and benefits are important for driving performance and retention, but intrinsic factors like passion, personal fulfillment, and a sense of purpose can help sustain long-term engagement and productivity. So, when thinking about motivation, it's about aligning external rewards with internal passions to maintain a high level of performance.

Asking the Right Questions

Neglecting middle managers' strengths or focusing on negative attributes and weaknesses create conditions of failure harmful to employees and organizations. Instead, **senior executives can consider the following questions** to facilitate their interactions with middle managers and choose a motivational approach that leverage the strengths of middle managers and align them with the goals and strategies of the organization.

Socio-psychological questions. These questions delve into how social contexts, relationships, and cultural norms influence middle managers' drive and goals, exploring issues like social comparison, achievement motivation, and the impact of group dynamics on behavior.

- How do social comparisons (e.g., using analogies to compare middle managers to others) impact the middle manager's motivation and self-perception?
- To what extent does the desire to fit in or stand out influence their behavior?
- How do cultural norms and leadership expectations shape middle managers' growth goals and career aspirations?
- How does frontline engagement of executives affect middle managers' morale and work motivation?
- What are the effects of major disruptions on middle managers' ability to meet their professional and growth goals?
- How do executives' perceptions of fairness and equity affect their views of middle managers' motivation?
- Where in the hierarchy of needs is the middle manager?
  - Are basic physiological needs being met?
  - Do middle managers have financial security?
  - Do they need emotional support? Do they have a sense of belonging?
  - Do they feel respected and trusted?

- Do we (senior executives) understand their long term goals and career aspirations?

Extrinsically motivated questions. These questions explore external rewards and incentives, such as asking about desired compensation, promotion opportunities, or recognition for achievements. Compensation and Benefits:

- What salary ranges are middle managers looking for in their roles?
- What benefits are most important for them?
- Dealing with disruptive technologies requires increased communication, upskilling, and potentially extra hours to navigate transitions and ensure psychological safety for everyone involved. How do middle managers feel about the current compensation and benefits package?
- Can the compensation of middle managers be aligned with the financial performance of the firm or to their unique contribution to the financial performance of the firm?

Leadership-motivated questions. These questions assess the ability of middle managers to inspire, influence, and drive their teams toward achieving goals and organizational objectives, focusing on their leadership skills and behaviors. They help executives understand how middle managers lead, rather than just what they think they should do.

- Are middle managers employing innovative approaches to team leadership?
- Are they considered trustworthy leaders by frontline employees?
- Do I (the senior executive) create sufficient opportunities for empowering them? Give them more autonomy in decision-making?

- Do middle managers inspire and motivate their teams and frontline leaders? Set clear goals and expectations? Delegate effectively?
- Do they get sufficient resources from me (the executive) to manage performance and provide feedback to team members?
- Do I provide them with opportunities to join the leadership development pipeline?
- Are middle managers considered for succession? Do I sponsor them? Provide sufficient coaching and guidance?

Senior executives can take proactive steps to fund the development of targeted training programs for middle managers that focus on strategic thinking, problem-solving, and leadership skills. Middle managers with strategy and leadership skills can help them gain a broader understanding of the organization's direction. Creating a culture where middle managers feel comfortable asking questions and providing feedback can help them to learn and grow. At the same time, it will give them the confidence and resources to make decisions, develop their strategic acumen, as well as enhance the talent of their direct reports.

Considerations for Middle Managers

It is vital that middle managers take proactive steps to communicate their indispensability to senior executives. They need to take the vision and goals of senior executives and cascade them appropriately so that frontline teams are aligned with that vision. Davenport and Harding (2010) recommended that middle managers become *off-stage managers* who focus on managing the environment, not the people. The off-stage manager creates an enabling and empowering environment where frontline teams and employees are entrusted with discretionary power to identify issues and solutions.

When middle managers shift their focus to influencing processes and decisions, not controlling them, their credibility is heightened, and trust is preserved. Sliding up to a governance role or down to an advocacy role, for example, could allow middle managers to use their dual roles up and down the hierarchy flexibly, especially during transitions. Strategies for self-development include the following:

1. *Take responsibility for your success and for your career.* Identify gaps in knowledge and skills you need to perform at a higher level and take proactive steps to close these gaps.
2. *Seek out an active sponsor.* Find a senior executive or a board director who can become your role model and, at the same time, facilitate your communications with C-group members as well as your path towards senior leadership positions.
3. *Take the initiative.* Seek out opportunities, propose new projects and improve work processes and systems. Build your reputation as an entrepreneurial thinker. Become an industry innovator by pioneering ideas and new products or services.
4. *Achieve more results than others.* Identify one or two areas within your position or department where you can make a significant impact within a short period of time.
5. *Know how to facilitate team interactions.* Every team is charged with a particular task and follows certain human and operational dynamics. Acquire emotional intelligence and project management skills that transcend a range of leadership qualities and that facilitate your work with different teams. Show your authentic self. Use empathy to gain trust up and down the chain of command.

6. *Become solution oriented.* Hold a positive, problem-solving, and enthusiastic attitude when working with peers and senior executives. Present solutions to senior leadership with a robust rationale and give credit to the people who contribute insights and ideas.
7. *Think and act like an executive.* Develop a matrix mind with multidimensional thinking. Use an outside-in perspective by incorporating the goals of external stakeholders in your thinking and decisions.

Middle managers are the key link between the strategic vision set by senior leadership and the daily operations carried out by their teams. They need to understand their organization's overall strategy and translate it into concrete actions and goals for their departments or teams, ensuring that everyone is aligned and working toward the same goals. When executives exclude middle managers from strategic and decision-making loops, it can lead to feelings of isolation, decreased morale, and ultimately hinder effective execution of strategies. The feelings of being undervalued or underappreciated are carried over and could lead to anxiety and depression or even to the hyper-effective conundrum discussed earlier.

Succession

Roughly 15%–20% of middle managers are promoted to senior executive positions. Grooming middle managers for senior leadership positions makes sense. Middle managers who are appreciated and are also targeted for upward mobility are more satisfied, productive, and committed. This aligns well with senior executives' goal to reduce the financial burden of turnover, rising replacement costs, time lag due to retraining and by-product costs such as adverse employee dissatisfaction with new hires.

Signifying the problem is the fact that a leadership gap can be averted if leadership development programs and succession planning exist along with willingness by senior executives to recognize that middle managers matter and promote from within. These observations point to a critical area where succession planning practices can and should be improved – the CEO and the board need to initiate the selection of internal candidates and ensure their preparation to lead and manage organizational transitions.

Forbes' (2023) Coaches Council shared common challenges and important tips middle managers will need as they move up the ladder and what senior executives can do to help. These are listed below with our added suggestions and **insights aimed at you, the middle manager, who is transitioning** to a senior leadership role. You will find these suggestions helpful in broadening your perspective and enhancing your growth goals to hone skills in strategic thinking and executive leadership.

- *Navigating a shifting personal definition of success.* At the senior leadership level, personal success often means meeting expectations or accomplishing goals through others. Use emotional intelligence (EI) skills to build trust. Give credit where credit is due.
- *Receiving less feedback; feeling isolated.* Moving into a leadership team shifts the focus and type of interactions. There will be less dissent, less critique, less feedback and greater feelings of isolation. Identify someone you trust to become your "sounding board" who will listen to you without judgment, sharing their views and experiences, reveal your weaknesses, and allow you to explore new ideas and opportunities.
- *Moving into a visionary mindset.* Shifting the mindset from doing to planning and from acting to thinking and even conceptualizing new ideas or creating a compelling

vision for success. Remember, in your new senior role you will be expected to provide direction, inspire action, and foster a sense of purpose that aligns departments and teams across the organization. Step forward with bold ideas and invite peer executives (and even middle managers that you wish to sponsor now!) to diverge or even play the "devil's advocate" by challenging or questioning the dominant alternative or encourage more explorations.

- *Resetting expectations.* To effectively move up the chain, focus on exceeding expectations, demonstrating leadership qualities, and building strong relationships within the organization. Join leadership training and development to hone your leadership skills, focus on continuous learning, seek mentorship, and build a network among peer executives (and high-performing middle managers!) to focus on growth opportunities.
- *Avoiding imposter syndrome.* When climbing up the ladder, leaders often face challenges related to imposter syndrome, the persistent feeling of inadequacy despite evidence of competence, caused by feelings of self-doubt, inability to measure up to expectations, fear of failure, and rough time accepting praise. You (the middle manager who has been promoted) should recognize that these feelings are normal. Think of them as constructive tensions that increase your flow of adrenaline and that stimulate creative thinking and new ideas. Focus on your accomplishments and strengths. Seek out an active mentor to help externalize your fear and listen to your concerns. Prioritize learning and continuing growth in the new role. Become an engaged and trustworthy leader!
- *Finding deeper purpose and alignment.* Become an authentic leader by discovering your unique *True North* (George & Sims, 2007). Develop strong self-awareness skills by thinking introspectively and holistically.

- *Shifting to a strategic mindset.* The challenge is shifting from a day-to-day operational and technical mindset to a strategic one. Managers who were great at the core responsibilities of their previous jobs are expected to have "big picture" thinking and the ability to anticipate trends or changes from the broader context of the overall strategy.
- *Practicing patience.* Middle managers typically have a short-term perspective on action. They tend to see results immediately. Executives must adapt to working on longer-term projects, including system-level changes. Adopt a "view from the balcony" (Heifetz et al., 2009) by stepping back from the immediate action (the "dance floor") to gain a broader perspective of the bigger picture, enabling problem-solving communications and smart choices.
- *Adopting a holistic organizational perspective.* The challenge for new executives is to transition from a departmental focus to a more holistic approach that considers the entire organization. Rotate through different departments to gain exposure to different aspects of the business, learn new skills, and develop a broader perspective. This helps to bridge departmental gaps and make decisions with the entire organization in mind.
- *Getting out of the weeds.* New executives need to stop managing daily activities, overseeing trivial tasks and putting out small fires. Transitioning away from managing daily activities requires strategic delegation, focusing on high-level tasks, and prioritizing time management to optimize and allow for more strategic thinking and leadership.
- *Learning to take calculated risks.* At the executive level, you (the promoted middle manager!) must understand the organization's overall risk tolerance, considering factors like financial stability, growth objectives, and industry dynamics. New executive-level leaders can help the

company reach new heights if they are aware of their options and test new assumptions and take wisely calculated risks based on analytics. For example, adopting new technologies can disrupt existing processes, but also lead to increased efficiency and competitiveness.

- *Having a Transition Plan.* Having a detailed transition plan is one of the most effective ways to set a new executive up for success. During the first several weeks, observe, ask questions, review expectations, meet people, identify opportunities, and start to set direction at a strategic level. At the same time, you should solicit ongoing support from peer executives to ensure a smooth and impactful integration into the new role.

Conclusion

How do organizations successfully cope with the increasing pace of disruptive technologies and digital transformation if their backbone, middle management responsible for knowledge transfer and innovation implementation, is removed from the decision-making process or are being circumvented? Middle managers matter as they have the know-how to carry out strategy and deliver results.

Including successful middle managers in the leadership talent pipeline adds significant value by fostering a strong, diverse, and prepared leadership team, ensuring leadership continuity, and driving innovation and growth. HR plays a critical role in creating best practices that empower, retain, and incentivize middle managers. It is very important to know how to appropriately judge the middle manager in ways that are fair and just to avoid undo bias. Coaching and mentoring programs have also been known to help cultivate more effective middle managers.

The inclusion of middle managers in decision-making, leadership development programs, and succession planning have been found to be lacking. Senior executives are not placing enough emphasis on cultivating the next cadre of leaders that will be required to sustain competitive advantage and business continuity. Often the importance of closed circle decision making and strategizing is prioritized by top executives who leave overwhelmed middle managers tied to tasks and operational issues, without the opportunity to step forward and exhibit their strategic acumen as the bridge between strategy and execution.

Middle managers are responsible for ensuring that the strategic plan is effectively implemented, which requires understanding the impact of constraints on strategy, identifying threats and opportunities, reviewing strengths and weaknesses, and developing measures to address disruptions and challenges head on.

With rising executive turnover rates, senior executives need to develop adequate succession programs to identify and train new leaders. Moreover, these programs should build a strong talent pipeline with those already working within the organization, especially since it costs less to develop and retain leaders in-house than to hire and train new managers. Senior executive talent can be challenging to find and promoting from within is usually the best strategy as it can also show female and male rising stars that career progression all the way to senior executive positions is possible.

References

Belasen, A. & Belasen, A. R. (2016). Value in the middle: Cultivating middle managers in healthcare organizations. *Journal of Management Development*, 35(9), 1149–1162.

Belasen, A. T. & Belasen, A. R. (2017). Strengthening the middle line: Overcoming motivational gaps, supporting promising managers, Best Paper, *Proceedings of the Seventy-Seventh Annual Meeting of the Academy of Management.* Online ISSN: 2151–6561. https://doi.org/10.5465/AMBPP.2017.7.

Belasen, A. & Frank, N. M. (2004). The perceptions of human resource managers of the shifting importance of managerial roles in downsizing organizations, *International Journal of Human Resources Development and Management*, 4(2), 144–163.

Belasen, A. & Luber, E. (2017). Innovation implementation: Leading from the middle out. In Nicole Pfeffermann & Julie Gould (Eds.), *Strategy and Communication for Innovation* (3rd ed.). Heidelberg, Germany: Springer.

Belasen, A. & Pfeffermann, N. (2024). *Brilliant Leadership – Unlocking the Power of Innovation-Communication.* Routledge.

Belasen, A. T. & Rufer, R. (2013). Innovation communication for effective inter-professional collaboration: A stakeholder perspective. In Nicole Pfeffermann, Tim Minshall, & Letizia Mortara (Eds.), *Strategy and Communication for Innovation* (pp. 227–240). Springer.

BLS. (2024). https://www.bls.gov/ooh/management/.

Davenport, T. & Harding, S. (2010). *Manager Redefined: The Competitive Advantage in the Middle of Your Organization.* Jossey-Bass.

Forbes. (2023). 15 challenges mid-level managers moving into executive leadership face, October 25. https://www.forbes.com/councils/forbescoachescouncil/2023/10/25/15-challenges-mid-level-managers-moving-into-executive-leadership-face/.

Gallup. (2024). Disruptive change is hitting leaders and managers hardest, May 23. https://www.gallup.com/workplace/645152/disruptive-change-hitting-leaders-managers-hardest.aspx#:~:text=Leaders%20and%20managers%20are%20more,teams%20working%20in%20different%20ways.

Gallup. (2023a). The manager squeeze: How the new workplace is testing team leaders, September 6. https://www.gallup.com/workplace/510326/manager-squeeze-new-workplace-testing-team-leaders.aspx.

Gallup. (2023b). The benefits of employee engagement, January 7. https://www.gallup.com/workplace/236927/employee-engagement-drives-growth.aspx.

George, B. & Sims, P. (Collaborator). (2007). *True North: Discover Your Authentic Leadership*. Jossey-Bass.

Heifetz, R. A., Linsky, M., & Grashow, A. (2009). *The Practice of Adaptive Leadership*. Harvard Business Review Press.

Letian, Z. (2023). The changing role of managers. *American Journal of Sociology*, 129(2), 439–484.

McKinney, R., McMahon, M., & Walsh, P. (2013). Danger in the middle: Why middle managers aren't ready to lead. *HBP Corporate Learning*, 1–8. http://www.harvardbusiness.org/sites/default/files/PDF/17807_CL_MiddleManagers_White_Paper_March2013.pdf.

McKinsey & Company. (2023). Investing in middle managers pays off—literally, June 26. https://www.mckinsey.com/capabilities/people-and-organizational-performance/our-insights/investing-in-middle-managers-pays-off-literally.

Osterman, P. (2009). *The Truth About Middle Managers: Who They Are, How they Work, Why They Matter*. Harvard Business School Press. https://hbr.org/podcast/2009/05/the-truth-about-middle-manager.

Prins, S. J., Bates, L. M., Keyes, K. M., & Muntaner, C. (2015). Anxious? depressed? you might be suffering from capitalism: Contradictory class locations and the prevalence of depression and anxiety in the USA. *Sociology of Health & Illness*, 37(8), 1352–1372.

Zenger, J. & Folkman, J. (2014). Why are middle managers so unhappy. *Harvard Business Review*, September 24. https://hbr.org/2014/11/why-middle-managers-are-so-unhappy.

Chapter 9

Rebranding Middle Managers

Introduction

This is the concluding chapter which recaps many of the ideas, lessons, and best practices discussed throughout the book. Middle managers are caught between a rock and a hard place. Mediating the workflow between strategic and operational levels, they face the challenge of balancing competing expectations vying for priority from both senior executives and direct reports. Navigating the dual role of directing teams and guiding the process of putting a plan into action is demanding, especially during implementation of disruptive technologies with rising tensions and difficult choices.

Surprisingly, however, despite their valuable contributions that often have gone unnoticed by senior executives, middle managers have regularly been perceived as nonessential assets that consume resources but do not add value to products or services. Viewed primarily as an expendable commodity that adds complexity and that hinders senior executives' ability to understand what is really going on at the frontline, middle

DOI: 10.4324/9781003608028-9

managers are kept out of the loop or bypassed (Belasen & Belasen, 2016).

Rapidly changing environments encourage executives to get closer to the frontline because it provides them with valuable, firsthand insight into customer needs, a better understanding of operational challenges, as well as solicit perspectives from frontline employees. Getting closer to the frontline allows executives to make more informed decisions based on unfiltered information and accelerates the pursuit of business goals. Further, as technology advances and social media allows executives to interact more directly with consumers and stakeholders, the strategy of thinning out the layers of management or 'unbossing' by removing middle managers from the supervision structure has gained popularity with senior executives.

This strategy slashes the number of administrative layers, flattens the hierarchy and effectively gives frontline leaders more autonomy and direct access to senior leadership. Frontline leaders who manage a large portion of the workforce are the critical linchpin for boosting team performance, enhancing resilience, and driving change. These leaders possess the functional knowledge and technical skills to execute business strategies without central oversight as time-to-market and quick responses during disruptions have greater impact on business success.

This presents critical challenges to sustainable growth. If senior executives, the planners, and frontline employees, the doers, communicate expectations or share the results of operations directly, who other than middle managers can better align complex tasks that require coordination across functional areas? If middle managers are perceived as nonvalue assets whose time in their roles expired, who else in the organization can link resources and capabilities across the internal supply chain, the interconnected processes and activities within a company responsible for delivering a product or service to the end users, to achieve organizational goals?

Unintended Consequences

Perceiving middle managers as intermediaries that slow operational efficiency without adding much measurable value has taken its toll on middle managers. Conscious about the potential of being eliminated, demoted, or bypassed, some middle managers attempt to "demonstrate their premium" by working excessively hard, becoming hypereffective (Belasen & Frank, 2004). Pressure to increase personal value and revalidate their worth to the organization comes from the commitment to perform their roles better, but also from the need to pick up the slack left by those who remain uninvolved or are forced to let go.

Senior executives may pay a price, too, as they unintentionally encourage employees to bypass middle managers, creating the potential for bottlenecks and information overload, interface confusion, and decreased productivity. Bypassing middle managers creates communication gaps, hinders operational efficiency, impacts employee morale, and potentially leads to poor execution of strategies.

Opportunity costs are high, too, as executives may miss out on leading and managing strategic initiatives and ensuring the long-term success of the organization. Given the magnitude of change, integration of AI technologies, and shifts in supply chains toward more localized sourcing strategies to mitigate disruption risks, withholding critical information from middle managers can be too costly. Senior executives lack the functional knowledge, time, or skills to translate high-level plans into actionable tasks without a middle management layer to facilitate this process (Belasen & Pfeffermann, 2024).

WHEN EMPLOYEES DISTRUST THEIR LEADERS

It's no surprise that, in the face of neglect, they overwhelmingly reported feeling invisible and frustrated, as well as burned out and powerless. The responses of the middle managers we surveyed laid bare what's driving their discontent and exposed the systemic issues that can no longer be ignored (FastCompany, 2024).

Surviving middle managers work more and produce more while receiving the same pay and, often, do so without any recognition of their accomplishments. Others inherit more tasks and greater variety but with routine responsibilities that require monitoring, not necessarily decision-making. They feel increasingly isolated from the management team, lose confidence in their abilities and, uncertain about their roles, often respond by shifting commitments. It is the diminished role in decision-making – the freedom to determine "how to get there," the making of the decision, not the execution – that is demoralizing.

Trapped in the middle, absent the psychological safety net, a necessity for personal security and self-confidence, these overworked and underappreciated managers are left with limited decision-making power and with increased levels of burnout and anxiety that overwhelm their cognitive abilities and significantly impair their ability to perform optimally.

Senior executives who react harshly to these attitudes and behaviors add fuel to the fire by typecasting middle managers as being unmotivated and needing to be further bypassed or often incentivized monetarily to accomplish important tasks (Belasen & Belasen, 2017).

CHALLENGES OF MIDDLE MANAGERS

Our research identified that 86% of high-potential employees feel burned out. That rate has climbed 59% since before the pandemic... On a high level, middle managers must act as mentors that drive and adapt to change, ensuring that the business operates like a well-oiled machine from the inside out. These individuals bridge the gap between frontline and executive leaders, unifying the company. Executives rely on them to deliver measurable outcomes. Peers look to them for support and collaboration. Direct reports expect them to give purpose, direction, and motivation. If middle managers freeze, an organization's strategic and cultural progress comes to a halt (DDI, 2022).

Smart executives who understand that work units and teams operate in environments that are largely influenced by broader strategic goals where middle managers are most needed for guiding and directing others, also recognize the need to leverage middle managers' strengths, especially when it comes to shifting between transformational and transactional roles.

Transformational and Transactional Roles

Middle managers perform transformational (big picture) and transactional (surface level) roles concurrently. Transformational roles drive employee motivation, engagement, and commitment to go beyond their self-interest and focus on the organization and the greater community. They inspire people to think from the balcony – to step back from a situation and take a broader, panoramic view of issues and underlying patterns. Transactional roles, however, focus on the orderly accomplishment of tasks and work activities, largely with an immediate or short-term focus. They stimulate employees, peers, and supervisors to think pragmatically – to consider a situation or problem from the ground level, focusing on the practical details and immediate realities rather than abstract or high-level thinking. While the transformational leader focuses on the people who perform the work, the transactional leader focuses on getting things done (Belasen et al., 2013).

As Figure 9.1 illustrates, while middle managers believe that, on balance, they perform the critical roles needed to support operations, senior executives think that they need to shift their focus away from external (markets, strategies) to internal operations (people, processes, structures, coordination). Further, senior executives perceive middle managers as lacking the ability to focus on the big picture without having the ability to connect the dots (Figure 9.2). Further, they often perceive them as circulating ideas without the ability to solve problems since they lack the skills or resources to effectively implement those ideas and achieve desired outcomes. They are perceived as incompetent, lacking the interface knowledge

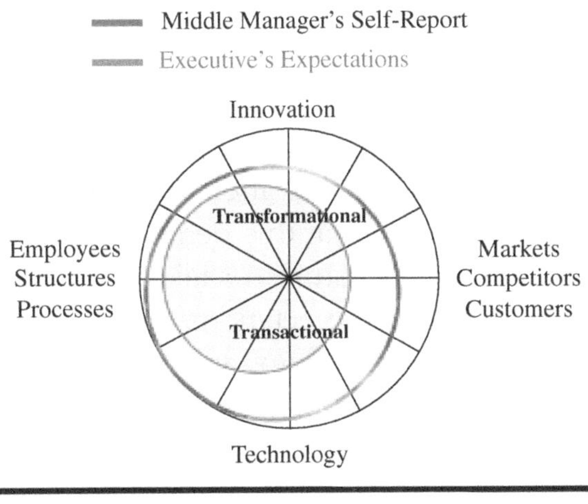

Figure 9.1 Perceptual Gap

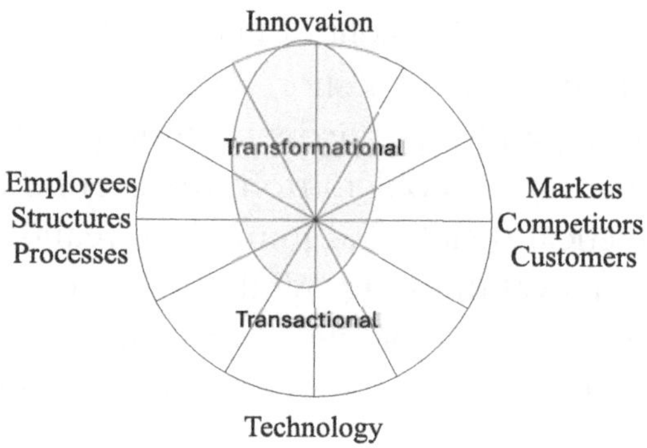

Figure 9.2 The Conceptual Middle Manager

and the critical thinking to figure out the feasibility of the ideas.

Conceptualizing change and innovation but without the ability to bring things to closure, keeps ideas and suggestions in the open without "how to" guidelines, plans, or explanations that provide advice, recommendations, or instructions. In that context, they inspire others through intangible concepts like shared values and creative thinking, rather than relying heavily on concrete details or implementation steps. They use big words to appear more intelligent, sophisticated, or authoritative, sometimes at the expense of clear communication, or a realistic view of what needs to be done. They often prioritize long-term goals, communicate the importance of agility but without a clear structure or concern for details.

Often middle managers are perceived as using excess empathy (Figure 9.3) that draws attention to their caregiving style without any concern that this behavior may lead employees to exploit their "good nature" or take advantage of them by lowering performance expectations or by compromising work schedules. Over-empathizing with employees by becoming too emotional or overly sensitive also leads to unintended biases when managers are perceived as weak or too submissive.

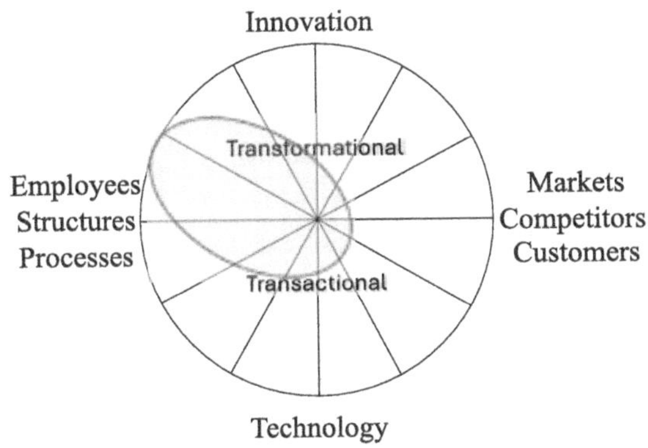

Figure 9.3 The Hyperempathic Middle Manager

Over-doing empathy may also lead to unbalanced decision making based on emotion rather than critical thinking – a perception triggered by executives who perceive middle managers as weak or hyperempathic (Figure 9.3). These managers may sacrifice accountability in favor of compassionate empathy without worrying about objectivity or by becoming too permissive with employees. Middle managers with excess empathy may absorb or take on emotions of others without setting boundaries or restrictions. They make decisions impulsively based on immediate emotions, without carefully weighing facts, logic, and potential consequences.

Middle managers are viewed as micromanagers, pencil pushers who prioritize power, demand compliance, and resort to hierarchical relations to make unilateral decisions (Figure 9.4). While these perceptions may be wrong, they are also beliefs held by senior executives who rationalize the need to thin out the supervision structure in the organization, in effect flattening the hierarchy. They see middle managers as "control freaks" who re-manage the functions below them without adding any significant value to the organization, hampering the ability of frontline leaders to maximize their potential and perform uninterruptedly.

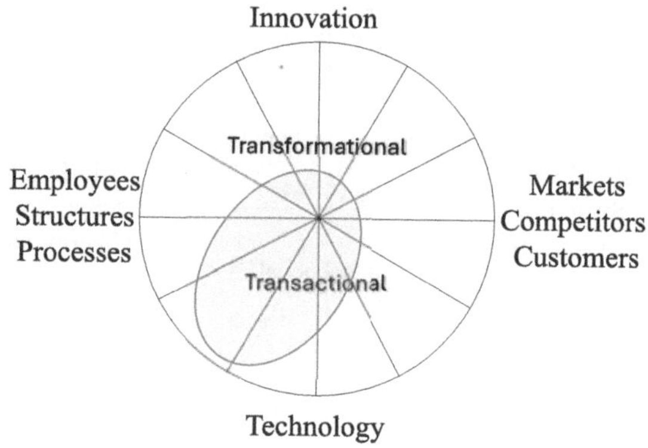

Figure 9.4 The Middle Micromanager

The insecurity that creeps up on middle managers and feeds into their cognition turns into a protective instinct in which they overcompensate for their feelings of mistrust through excess monitoring and redundant supervision regardless of how important the tasks are. This vicious cycle of excess control further fuels the perception of rigid managers and displaced leaders whose role in the organization has reached its limits.

Middle managers are perceived as power-hungry managers who have an excessive need for power or authority (Figure 9.5). They create a circle of loyal staff who shield them from others and are hostile toward those who oppose them. These managers are viewed as self-centered individuals who flex their muscles by making decisions unilaterally with limited employee engagement. They use information selectively and avoid giving feedback that does not fit with their priorities or interests.

Fearing retribution or abuse of power causes direct reports to lay low or bypass middle managers by moving up-and-down the hierarchy. Meanwhile senior executives' views of middle managers' nonvalue are reinforced with concerns of stifled creativity, poor decision-making, a lack of accountability, decreased morale, and resistance to innovation

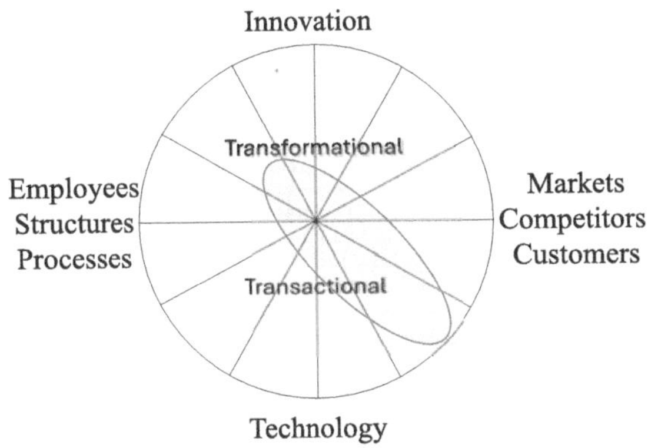

Figure 9.5 The Autocratic Middle Manager

implementation, as frontline leaders may be less likely to voice concerns or dissent due to the power imbalance generated by middle managers.

Rebranding Middle Managers

The key is to rebrand the role of middle managers from a liability to an asset by recognizing their strategic value to the organization. But this will occur only if senior executives recognize the value proposition of middle management and take steps to bridge the trust gap between the two levels.

Senior executives need to focus on reinforcing the critical role of middle managers as strategic communicators, expert team builders and motivators, change champions, and facilitators who translate a high-level vision into actionable plans that frontline leaders and employees can understand. Empowering middle managers to play a more active role in decision-making and in the execution of strategies contributes to the credibility of senior executives and to the overall success of the organization.

An important responsibility for senior executives is to set up a targeted development program for identifying and cultivating the leadership talent pipeline to ensure a continuous stream of qualified leaders to meet the evolving needs of the business (Belasen & Pfeffermann, 2024). As part of a reliable succession plan, this program should include sponsorship, active mentoring, and foster a culture of continuous learning and internal mobility that prepares middle managers for senior leadership roles.

To thrive in the digital-transformative era, senior executives who recognize the viability of a culture of trust, also rely on middle managers for translating organizational strategy into feasible tasks, and for their know-how to integrate people and work units and to evaluate the impact of change on customers, partners, stakeholders, and employees. These are the middle managers who possess a deep understanding of a company's history, processes, culture, and key relationships – the institutional memory – the collective set of facts, concepts, best practices, and skills essential for knowledge transfer and innovation implementation (Belasen & Bertola, 2024).

An organization that empowers its middle managers allows for greater diversity of viewpoints. While senior executives are too distant, middle managers are closer to frontline employees, able to leverage informal networks, and let employees feel valued and not alienated. Middle managers can draw ideas and suggestions from their direct reports and share interpretations or practical implications for advancing business objectives, prioritizing tasks, or rebalancing short- and long-term objectives with top executives. Evidence shows that middle managers' upward leadership and downward influence affect the alignment of organizational activities with strategic intents. They help facilitate innovation solutions by managing up and implementing innovation by leading and guiding teams and employees (Belasen & Luber, 2017).

YOUR MOST PRECIOUS RESOURCE: MIDDLE MANAGERS

Middle management is a vital yet beleaguered role within organizations. Managers face pressures from above and below, they tend to be both underdeveloped and unempowered, and they face growing pressure to deliver in flatter, faster, and leaner organizational structures, all of which leads to being underutilized and unappreciated. The findings of a new McKinsey Global Survey of middle managers suggest that many companies may be unintentionally thwarting middle managers' ability to perform in their roles. Companies treat middle management as a catchall, requiring managers to spend much of their time handling nonmanagerial work and navigating organizational bureaucracy rather than allowing them to focus on the most important role at an organization: fostering talent (McKinsey, 2023).

Dual Role and Disruptive Innovation

Implementing innovation often involves a dual role: balancing the need to exploit existing strengths and resources (exploitative innovation) with the need to explore new possibilities and create disruptive change (exploratory innovation). Exploitative innovation focuses on improving and refining existing products, processes, or services to achieve incremental gains and efficiency. It leverages established knowledge and capabilities to optimize current operations and maintain a competitive edge in the existing market.

Exploratory innovation involves venturing into new areas, exploring uncharted territories, and developing entirely new products, services, or business models. It requires a willingness to take risks and embrace uncertainty, potentially leading to significant breakthroughs and disruption.

Successful organizations recognize the importance of both types of innovation and strive to balance them effectively. They develop the strategies and processes that allow them to both exploit their strengths and to explore new opportunities, ultimately leading to sustainable growth and competitive advantage over their rivals. Examples of dual innovation include the following.

- A company might focus on improving its existing manufacturing processes (exploitative) while simultaneously investing in research and development for new materials or technologies (exploratory).
- A retailer might optimize its online store for better customer experience (exploitative) while also exploring new delivery methods or personalized shopping experiences (exploratory).

Benefits of dual innovation include the following.

- *Increased Competitiveness*: By combining the strengths of both exploitative and exploratory innovation, organizations can stay ahead of the curve and maintain a competitive edge.
- *Enhanced Resilience*: A dual-innovation approach allows organizations to adapt to changing market conditions and disruptions by leveraging both existing strengths and new capabilities.
- *Sustainable Growth*: By continuously innovating, organizations can drive long-term growth and create new value for their customers and stakeholders

Implementing innovation requires an effective balance of strategic awareness with operating experience and an optimal mix of leadership and management roles. This is important since middle managers more so than senior executives or frontline supervisors have the competence needed to handle the complexity of disruptive innovation.

High-impact middle managers optimize their value by facilitating adaptation using transformational roles and by implementing deliberate strategy using transactional roles. As Figure 9.6 shows, middle managers operate at the nexus between leadership and management and align internal capabilities and resources with the opportunities and challenges presented in the external environment. This strategic approach helps organizations optimize their performance by leveraging strengths, mitigating weaknesses, capitalizing on opportunities, and navigating threats. Middle managers internalize the stress not only between leadership and management goals and methods but also between loyalty to the company's goals and objectives, interests, and needs of customers. This is where leadership strengths, the fine communication skills that high impact middle managers develop over time, come into play as they seek to accomplish integrative solutions.

Middle managers are not just the support system on which an organization pivots. Importantly, they serve as the lynchpin that at times of disruption holds the organization together

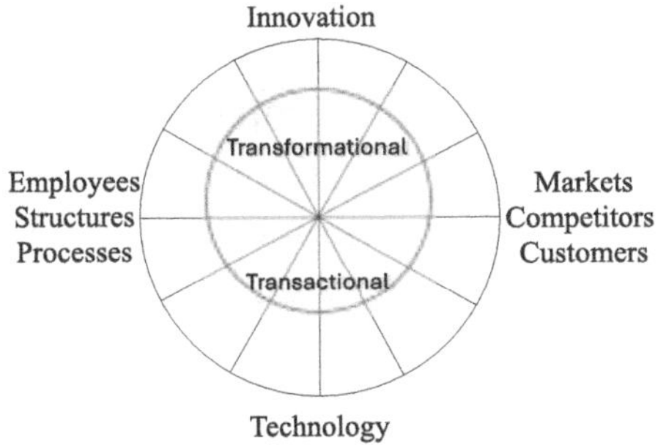

Figure 9.6 Balanced Leadership

when it is pulled in different directions (e.g., by marketing and operations or manufacturing and sales). When it comes to disruptive innovation, middle managers have the know-how to build resilience and develop new capabilities that enable sound operations and that deliver reliable products and services to the market.

Facilitating adaptability requires that the middle managers relax control to get new projects started, secure time for experimental programs, locate and provide resources for trial projects, and encourage informal discussion and information sharing. They can implement the intended strategy by communicating and clarifying objectives to lower levels, translating goals into action plans, and monitoring essential project activities, costs, and milestones. When project quality and reliability requirements are achieved, middle managers shift their predominant style "directing" to "steering," becoming team leaders and team advocates, providing feedback, building trust, and cultivating a collaborative work environment.

The same way that middle managers balance the needs of talent versus corporate objectives; they must balance the corporate identity against the brand promises and the company's sense of responsibility against its earnings consistency. Their "why" is encapsulated in the following question: *Are the employees delivering the brand experience promised on the company's advertising channels?*

Thus, not only do middle managers play a significant role in implementing innovation, but they align company messages so that the market credits the company with receiving and delivering the innovation. Middle management helps make innovation happen for the customer and enables the company to sustain its reputational assets externally.

Profile Awareness

Aspiring middle managers with a continuing growth mindset have an authentic personality, empathy to engage individuals and teams, the ability to facilitate cocreation, inspire others, and they commit to making significant contributions to their organizations. They are aware of their vulnerabilities and have the humility to defer to experts or delegate responsibilities to competent team members. Integrating vulnerabilities into the range of their behaviors enhances their perceived integrity and trustworthiness and reflects dependability that not only reinforces leadership attributes of transparency, accountability, credibility, and honesty but also promote followers' preference to work with middle managers that are both authentic and trustworthy.

Self-aware leaders reflect on their personal strengths and weaknesses, are sensitive to how others interpret their words and actions and have an aptitude for learning from mistakes so they can perform their roles more effectively. Strong self-awareness is linked to high self-regulation or personal control that helps leaders act on strengths in guiding individuals and teams and in pursuing positive outcomes.

To foster the alignment between actual behaviors and expectations from others, assessment instruments can be used to identify weaknesses and develop ways to bridge possible gaps. Another option is to obtain feedback from others (e.g., stakeholders, executives, board members, direct reports) about how well middle managers meet expectations. A gap analysis could then reveal areas for further development. Ideas and actions for improvement or self-development could be prioritized to reflect inputs from others and eventually lead to a better alignment between the leader's self-perceptions and perceptions by others. One such instrument appears below.

The 32-item survey includes a 5-point Likert-type scale response options ranging from 1 (I do not demonstrate this behavior) to 5 (demonstrate this behavior to a great extent) to score the individual items. Rate each item on a scale from 1 to 5 where:

1 – I do not demonstrate this behavior
2 – I demonstrate this behavior to a small degree
3 – I demonstrate this behavior to a moderate degree
4 – I demonstrate this behavior frequently
5 – I demonstrate this behavior to a great extent

Respondents can answer the survey questions twice – as a manifestation of their "actual" behavior and second, as a reflection of how they would like to be perceived by others (desired). Others may include specific categories of people or list of people that interact with you on a regular basis – peers, direct reports, and/or supervisors.

Innovation

1. I have the skills to initiate innovation
2. I help employees understand the importance of disruptive innovation
3. Others know where I stand on change issues
4. I am interested in obtaining insights from others
5. Diverse group members provide multiple perspectives on action
6. I pursue disruptive innovation
7. I encourage risk-taking and experimentation
8. I promote entrepreneurial thinking

Competition

9. My values are aligned with strategic goals
10. We establish brand recognition by gaining a competitive edge
11. I know how to move quickly and bring individuals and teams on board
12. I know what consumers in our target market think about our brand
13. I promote the use of disruptive technology to penetrate new markets
14. We have high confidence in repositioning the organization
15. We build strong customer relationships
16. I help create brand loyalty and increase the likelihood of repeat purchases

Technology

17. I use AI technology to integrate the value chain
18. I know how to scale innovation
19. I am engaged in innovation implementation
20. Our stakeholders perceive us as an innovative organization
21. I understand and support digital transformations
22. I guide individuals and teams about advances in technology
23. I embrace collaborative technologies across the organization
24. I promote investments in hiring, growing, and retaining talent analytics

Social

25. Employees view me as a trustworthy innovator
26. I have high tolerance for ambiguity
27. I am open to feedback even if it is negative
28. I reveal my weaknesses to others
29. I reward innovative ideas and efforts
30. I influence my organization to empower change agents
31. I have the know-how to mobilize support for change
32. I have strong project management skills

A deficiency in the ***innovation dimension*** (Figure 9.7) creates a perception of middle managers as rigid with a reluctance to consider alternative perspectives. These managers rely on a narrow approach of management which prefers routine, tradition, and familiarity over novelty and change. Middle managers with low propensity for openness may resist new ideas, avoid challenges, withhold information, and struggle to adapt during disruptions.

They might also have narrow interests in new technologies and find complex or ambiguous situations challenging, often avoiding situations that disrupt their comfort zones or

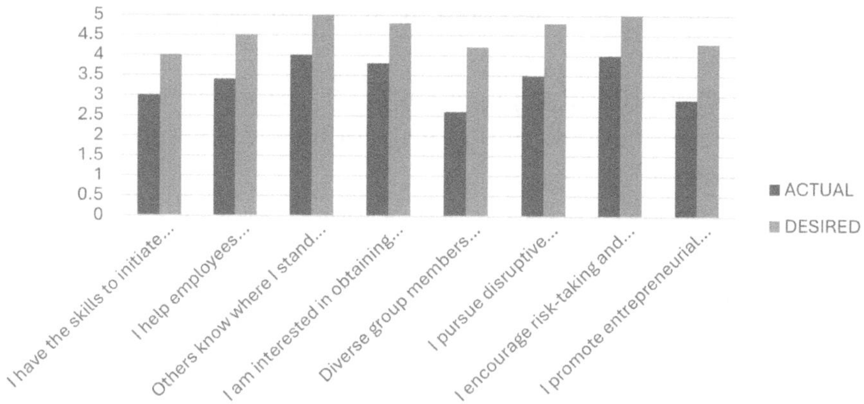

Figure 9.7 Innovation

established routines. Feeling comfortable with the status quo, they tend to pass up opportunities for personal or professional growth that involve change or new challenges. When left underdeveloped, middle managers may be hesitant to embrace new ideas, AI technologies, or innovative approaches to leading change, preferring to stick with what they already know – the current status quo. When others offer insights and ideas, they tend to bunker down or settle in a safe place or wait for the storm or disruption to dissolve. Instead, successful middle managers with strengths in this dimension use creative thinking to stimulate further reactions or optimal solutions, are receptive to learning from new experiences or perspectives, potentially broadening their overall development.

A potential deficiency in the ***competition dimension*** (Figure 9.8) occurs when a middle manager is too inwardly focused, paying attention to operational issues, as well as to managing integration dynamics. While these are important matters and they cannot be ignored, the temptation is to act with a sense of urgency rather than strategy. Refocusing on purposeful ideas as the basis for strengthening strategic visioning, entrepreneurial thinking, and becoming a champion of change by embracing an industry mindset can help bridge

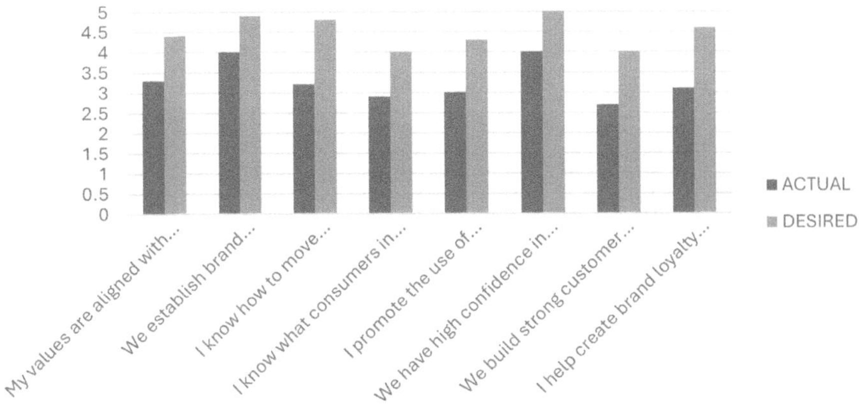

Figure 9.8 Competition

the gap between the actual and desired profiles. Embracing an industry mindset involves cultivating a growth mindset, staying adaptable, and continuously learning to thrive in a dynamic and evolving industry. It is about viewing challenges as opportunities, embracing diverse perspectives, and actively seeking feedback to improve industry positioning and market share.

A potential deficiency in the ***technology dimension*** (Figure 9.9) refers to areas where technological advancements or applications lag, leading to implementation challenges and missed opportunities across the organization. This can manifest as issues related to integration, access, lack of digital skills or training that hinder individuals' ability to effectively utilize technology, insufficient infrastructure, ethical considerations, misuse of technology such as the spread of misinformation. A typical gap occurs due to insufficient investment in professional development or a reluctance to embrace new technologies with either hindering progress or limiting the potential for innovation implementation, and suboptimal functioning within the socio-technological structures of the organization.

Middle managers whose ratings are relatively low on the ***social dimension*** (Figure 9.10) need to resist the temptation to make decisions quickly, even though the urgent pressures

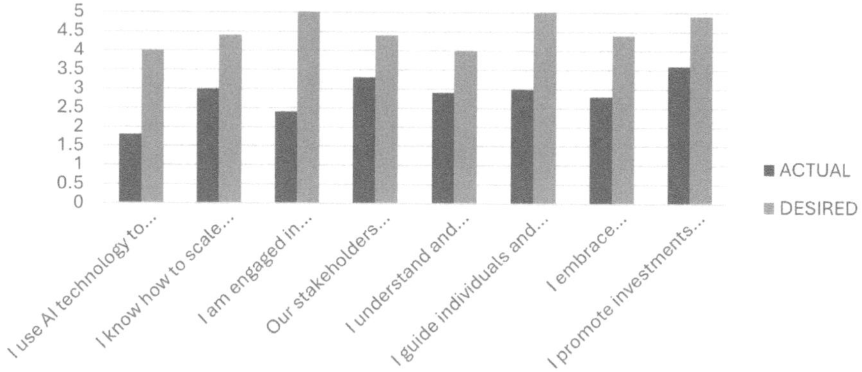

Figure 9.9 Technology

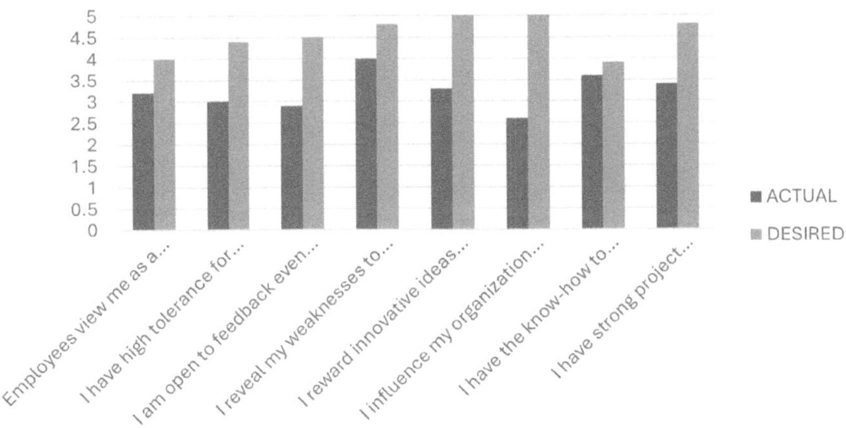

Figure 9.10 Social

of the moment may push them into deciding too quickly. As discussed earlier in this chapter, a weakness in this area is usually marked by a tendency to shoot from the hip, resulting in unilateral decisions without the benefit of input from affected people or without having all available information. Higher ratings, however, signify rising levels of integrity, empathy, and accountability for actions associated with desirable outcomes. Feedback from others can help guide middle managers about possible remedies and continuous improvement. Middle managers are expected to have strong emotional intelligence skills and the ability to use transparent communication with a focus on openness and honesty as great behavioral mitigators for building trust in organizations despite facing highly stressful situations.

Figure 9.11 transposes the actual and desired profiles to provide a single view of the gaps across the four dimensions of balanced leadership. The gap between the two profiles signifies opportunities for improvement. These aggregate profiles show a more "panoramic" view of the differences between actual and desired values and behaviors.

Self-improvement could be integrated into a leadership training and development program that more systematically

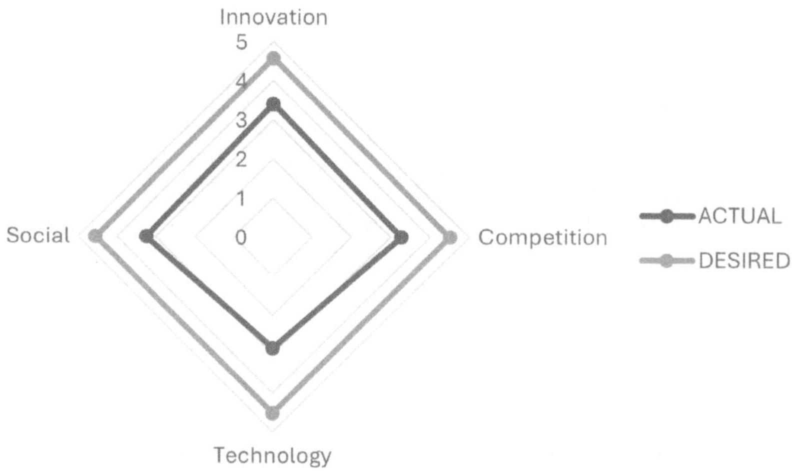

Figure 9.11 Composite Profile

can guide aspiring middle managers to pursue high performing leadership qualities. Middle managers hold the keys for successful innovation implementation. They are critical for integrating people and tasks, linking functional areas around common objectives, monitoring performance, and ensuring a reliable flow of resources to sustain the accomplishment of goals.

Senior executives who understand the value proposition of middle managers, know how to communicate with empathy and authenticity, engage middle managers in decision-making processes and provide them with the psychological safety, critical for sparking engagement and building trust in a purpose-driven workplace that connects employees to the "why" and that embodies the organization's purpose and values.

References

Belasen, A. T. & Belasen, A. R. (2016). Value in the middle: Cultivating middle managers in healthcare organizations. *Journal of Management Development*, 35(9), 1149–1162.

Belasen, A. T. & Belasen, A. R. (2017). Strengthening the middle line: Overcoming motivational gaps, supporting promising managers, Best Paper, *Proceedings of the Seventy-Seventh Annual Meeting of the Academy of Management.* Online ISSN: 2151–6561.

Belasen, A. T. & Bertola, L. (2024). Co-creation, strategic visioning, and iterative loops. Chapter 4 in Alan T Belasen & Nicole Pfeffermann (Eds.), *Brilliant Leadership – Unlocking the Power of Innovation-Communication* (pp. 63–77). New York, NY: Routledge.

Belasen, A. & Frank, N. M. (2004). The perceptions of human resource managers of the shifting importance of managerial roles in downsizing organizations. *International Journal of Human Resources Development and Management*, 4(2), 144–163.

Belasen, A. & Luber, E. (2017). Innovation implementation: Leading from the middle out. In Nicole Pfeffermann & Julie Gould (Eds.), *Strategy and Communication for Innovation: Integrative Perspectives on Innovation in the Digital Economy* (pp. 229–243). Germany: Springer.

Belasen, A. & Pfeffermann, N. (2024). *Brilliant Leadership – Unlocking the Power of Innovation-Communication.* New York, NY: Routledge.

Belasen, A., Eisenberg, B., & Rutigliano, K. (2013). Manage to lead, lead to manage: Integrating transformational leadership with transactional management. In Michele Paludi (Ed.), *Managing, Leading, and Developing Employees* (pp. 21–41). Santa Barbara, CA: Praeger.

DDI. (2022). Piggy in the middle: The challenges of middle management, October 19. https://www.ddiworld.com/blog/challenges-of-middle-management.

Fast Company. (2024). Here's what happens when employees don't trust their leadership, November 7. https://www.fastcompany.com/91222315/heres-what-happens-when-employees-dont-trust-their-leadership.

McKinsey. (2023). Stop wasting your most precious resource: Middle managers. https://www.mckinsey.com/capabilities/people-and-organizational-performance/our-insights/stop-wasting-your-most-precious-resource-middle-managers.

Index